THEY PROMISED US

THE MOON

AND THEN PROCEEDED TO GIVE EVERYTHING ELSE AWAY

BY

WILLIAM PARKER ARCHIBALD

They Promised Us the Moon

Textual Advisement: Elaine Bush
Technical Support: Digital Depot (Maurice Tift)
Editing: Kit Duncan
Book Layout: Nat Mara

A writer should struggle with the words
so the reader won't have to.

— the author

When I was a youngster,

My father's favorite joke was about the farmer who had a pig with a wooden leg. When asked about it, the farmer went on for days about the virtues of the pig and how attached the family had become to it.

Acknowledging all of that, the visitor asked yet again why the animal had a wooden leg. To which the farmer responded, "Well, if you had a pig like that, would you eat it all at once?"

This, in a real way, is the story of America. I'm not questioning our love for it. That is well established. Rather, I'm questioning why, after centuries of toil and sacrifice, we've all of a sudden turned on it and are now devouring it with the reckless abandon of fools who sat down to feast on the goose that laid the golden egg.

Dedication

This book, indeed this whole endeavor to preserve, protect and defend that which has been given to us at such enormous cost, is dedicated to all of the patriots, both living and dead and to my good friend and mentor,

**Millard Fuller,
founder of Habitat for Humanity International and the Fuller Center for Housing.**

Table of Contents

ELEVATOR

DOWN

1969 To the Present

There's no way that life should be this hard, not in this land, not in this time. At the end of the 1960's, beginning of the 1970's, this country was on top of the heap with no one remotely within striking distance. Oh sure, the Cold War was still raging, but we had touched down on the Moon just as communist Russia, crumbling under the weight of its own broken promises, was beginning its slow, downward spiral toward certain doom. Within two brief decades, once proud Soviet coal miners would be striking for something as basic as bar soap while people stood in endless lines for the few pieces of rotten produce on their grocers' shelves.

Americans, on the other hand, had good jobs, career positions with solid benefits and pensions. One person on a blue collar wage could feed an entire family, put the kids through college, own their home outright and retire young enough to travel the country in an RV. There was pride, there was hope, there was every expectation that the future would be even rosier and life all the easier. Why wouldn't it be? After all, they promised us the Moon.

Now look at us. If we haven't lost our job or home, or had our savings and hope of retiring wiped out, we know someone in our family or down the street that has. Just this week, I found a person living in his car at an interstate highway rest area. Friends and I are now scrambling to get him on his feet. This situation was simply unimaginable but a brief time ago.

Two Seminal Events

Two seminal events occurred. The first took place on July 21, 1969, when, in my opinion, America reached the apex of its ascendance by trouncing the Russians through winning the "space race." We were the first to make a manned lunar landing before returning safely home to planet Earth.

The second occurred just three years later in 1972, when Richard Nixon, aka "Tricky Dicky," in what the press dubbed his "greatest diplomatic achievement," opened the doors for trade with mysterious and secretive China.

The backdrop for this historic event was a much touted ping pong match between China's best players and ours. We may no longer remember who won that contest, but when we skip ahead to my local newspaper in August of 2011, it becomes clear that we lost far more than a game.

What, pray tell, was the big news in Americus, Georgia, that caught not only my eye but also the attention of NBC, CNN and *The Today Show*? It was only that China's ever increasing trade imbalance with the US now had a counterbalance. That's right, we finally had something they wanted and needed. You guessed it, chopsticks. China apparently has a shortage of lumber, so they started manufacturing them here in the USA.

The newspaper interviewed workers at the new Americus, Georgia, facility where I live. Virtually all of them stated how relieved they were to finally have a job, any job, in a community with shuttered factories and a 14% unemployment rate. They also repeatedly said that they saw this new plant as a definite step in the right direction. One televised version of the same event went even further. They added an important bit of information overlooked by my paper and most Americans.

While we were busy filling boxes with chopsticks for export to China, the Chinese exported something to us as well. It arrived in slightly larger containers.

They sent us a brand new Oakland Bay Bridge. That's right, the whole thing, stretching from one shore clear over to the other. It seems that California, with its record unemployment, saw fit to forego hiring its own people and decided instead to save money by purchasing an entire bridge from China. It consisted of nine segments spanning from Oakland to San Francisco.

In just a little over forty years, the United States has gone from being one of the wealthiest countries in the world to one of the most deeply indebted, while China, during the same period of time, rose from rice paddies to the world's largest exporter of consumer goods.

The History

What many of us forget is that when western television crews first went into China, the West was literally holding its breath, fearing the first images to beam back home to America would be those of people starving in the streets. That's how poor they were. They had nothing. They were penniless and little better off than the people of North Korea today. Their country had no rich mineral deposits, no silver and gold, nor any intellectual property worth marketing. They had nothing at all, just billions of people living a subsistence life under communism.

The obvious question is, what did they have that we wanted? The answer is sheer numbers. We didn't look at China as having the things we wanted. We looked at China as having the consumers we wanted. Coca Cola executives, to mention just one interest, were drooling over the prospect of having billions of people drinking Coke. After all, the American business model is simple: create a desire, then stoke the fire.

The problem was that a soft drink was ridiculously out of reach for the typical Chinese peasant – and that's what most of them were at that time, peasants living off the land. Undeterred, American corporations set up state-of-the-art factories that gave Chinese workers the money to purchase Coca Colas and other American goods. At the same time, this provided a vastly cheaper way for these corporations to make things, thanks to a much lower pay scale in China. These same products would then be shipped stateside where they clobbered competitors who still paid wages commensurate with supporting a typical American family. In response, companies back home, desiring to remain competitive in this new cost cutting environment, followed suit, shuttered their factories and joined the mad dash overseas.

To Recap

There we have it. We were riding high as a nation, but the captains of industry weren't satisfied. They wanted more, more profits and more money. The only way they could do it was to increase market share by selling us down the river. So what if Americans lost their jobs? They didn't care. They were putting money into the pockets of a new pool of potential consumers who would then, for the very first time, be able to buy their goods.

To sweeten the deal even more, these same captains of industry then turned around and made a dollar off the very economy they were destroying. Once proud American workers, now with less disposable income as all of the good (and even poor paying) jobs were fast disappearing, had little choice but to gobble down these cheap goods that began to pour into this country. In short, the greed of the few set off a chain of events that has bankrupted us as a nation and left us struggling at the very time we should be reaping the harvest of all those who worked so hard and sacrificed so much.

A Cancerous Growth

On the surface, it looked like growth and in a certain sense it was. Yet, it was a destructive growth, an out of control cancer, a ballooning tumor destroying everything in its path. Wal-Mart is a prime example of this dynamic. Yes, it shot up fast and grew like a weed, but it single handedly wiped out most small town business districts across the country, leaving them boarded up and desolate. High quality family run businesses where people were welcomed with a sincere, "How may I help you?" were replaced with impersonal big box stores employing disinterested greeters who were clueless about the thousands of square feet of low-end merchandise behind them. For the first time in America's history, the race wasn't to the top, but rather to the lowest level.

People were retooling their thinking away from asking how to better their position through innovation and improvement to the more insidious question of how to improve their position by getting their neighbor to surrender more and more. If the item or service cost X number of dollars, our question became the same as that asked by Wal-Mart, "Can you do it for less?"

Colonialism

When a developed world power, such as Great Britain, establishes a relationship of economic dominance over an undeveloped land, such as it did with the thirteen American colonies, it is called colonialism. Its intention is not to advance the weaker state, but rather to exploit it for its own benefit. It does this by dismantling or preventing the development of manufacturing facilities in the fledgling nation. This forces the weaker country to sell its raw materials to the dominant country (as it has nothing else to export). The proceeds from the sale of these raw materials are then used to purchase finished goods from the dominant country. This bleeds wealth from the weaker state and, in time, demoralizes its people as sooner or later they come to realize they have no hope for real advancement. Rather, they are trapped in a seemingly endless cycle of supplying both raw materials and a steady stream of customers to the very nation that has them in its grip.

Reverse Colonialism

In the forty plus years since opening the doors of trade with China, we in the US have witnessed, and indeed facilitated, a complete reversal of the above dynamic. For instead of creating more production jobs here and a global customer base to buy our goods, we have done just the opposite. We have laid off our own workforce, carted up the very machinery they were using, shipped it overseas and have become consumers of the goods we previously made here at home. Then, we find ourselves scratching our heads and wondering why we have shuttered factories, record unemployment and staggering trade deficits. It isn't rocket science, folks. The reason we have fewer jobs here is because we bundled them up with nice little ribbons and shipped them all overseas to China.

Now, the American worker is on the sidelines, watching economic reports on the news that no longer impact him or her. For even when recessions end and things do improve on Wall Street, the good news has little bearing on things here at home as the country is experiencing what the press has dubbed a "jobless recovery."

This means, as the label suggests, that even though demand is up and American corporations are turning in record profits, they aren't hiring people here at home, but rather they are hiring foreigners to work in facilities they have built overseas.

Reasons for Sending Factories to China

I. *We honestly believed we could do without them*. It was as though we bought into the notion that if we moved money around fast enough, it would somehow create sufficient inertia to keep the wind in our sails. Reality has proven this simply isn't the case. No matter how many times a slick bank ad refers to some new line of credit as a "product," the truth of the matter is that money is not and never has been a product. It is nothing more and nothing less than a marker for, or representative of, tangible goods and services. Money doesn't make money. People make the goods and produce the services that are measured in terms of dollars and cents.

II. *Arrogance. We thought "menial work" was beneath us*. If we had to produce anything, it would be high tech items like computer chips, jet engines or advanced medical imaging equipment. Unskilled labor in poorer nations would make mundane things like frying pans and dust mops. We would devote ourselves to the high end gadgetry that made the Silicon Valley famous.

(Obviously, this wasn't such a great idea.)

The problem, of course, is that electronics make up only a sliver of our Gross National Product (the sum total of all we produce). The lion's share consists of everyday things like bath towels, vacuum cleaners, ball point pens, and electrical outlet covers. These are what make or break an economy. Today, all of these items bear the label "Made in China" and increasingly, the high tech items do as well.

III. *Good Old Garden Variety Greed: "Let's get rich by making things cheaper in China!"* Out of a desire to make a quick buck, companies began producing items in China for less than 50 cents on the dollar and then transported them here for sale. Even after the cost of shipping them halfway around the world, they still enjoyed a much bigger profit than if they paid workers here to produce them. What they didn't figure was that in time, American wallets would run out of money to buy ironing boards as more and more of us got laid off. And now, while our economy is shrinking, China is enjoying record expansion. They not only profit from selling us all of those ironing boards that we previously made here, they also make interest on loans we've taken out to cover the lack of income we've suffered since laying ourselves off. It's beyond ludicrous. It's insane.

Thanks for your "New World Order" George (Bush I), but take it back; we're no longer going to fall for it!

Unless one's country is terribly small, like Monaco, or an island nation like Bermuda, most items for sale are generally produced right there in the home country by the citizens who use them. This only makes sense as it provides jobs and a stable base to the economy.

Yet, while most nations have been building up their industrial base, we've had the "New World Order" shoved down our throats by President after President from both parties. How's that been working out for us? Apparently, it's not been going too well. We've been in decline for decades. We've been able to mask it by first working more hours on the job, then taking on more jobs, then sending out more people from our households to do more work, but we still fall farther and farther behind.

The Myth Was That Globalization Would Increase Sales

In reality, other nations were already foaming at the mouth, saving every dime they could muster, just to purchase these very things that at one time were only produced here. Now, the very same inventions that were previously American-made are no longer headed for the docks of Oakland, California, Seattle, Washington, or Baltimore, Maryland, but rather to far off ports of call. We've turned the whole thing backwards. Computers and other high end products are now made overseas.

It's A Global Financial Shift, Not a Meltdown

When Democrats stick their heads out of the hole we've all dug together, they immediately notice a lack of jobs and incorrectly correlate it to the Great Depression. This is a really big, huge, gargantuan, monumental, running out of sufficient words to describe it, mistake. Why? Because, comparing what's going on to the1930's sets up a whole series of incorrect assumptions that lead to prescribing the wrong medicine.

To begin with, unlike the 1930's, this is not and never has been bad news for everyone. China and India are doing quite well, thank you. In fact, they are on an upward trajectory every bit as pronounced as the downward trend we're experiencing here. It's as though we're all on a great big economic teeter-totter and they are on the other end, going up just as we are coming down.

It's No Coincidence -
Their Rise Is Linked
To Our Decline

How could it be otherwise? We've given them everything they need to flourish, while at the same time, we've taken away all that has supported and protected us. For starters, we have handed over our advanced technology, not only in blueprints, but often in real time production capabilities as we sent the actual machines American workers were using to make our industries purr. Then, we took down reasonable trade barriers (that up until now have kept our wages and standard of living high), while at the same time giving competitors our "most favored nation status." This gives them an unfair advantage over the few American owned and operated factories that still remain. Then, to come full circle and complete the process, we have provided a steady stream of customers to buy their goods.

The second mistake that flows from correlating today's situation to a scaled back version of the Great Depression (where we assume the whole world is suffering – which again, isn't true) is to assume that only the government has deep enough pockets to stimulate growth by hiring people. This all sounds plausible, but none of it is accurate. The treasury might have deep pockets, but there are only holes in them. Not only doesn't the government have any money, it has also just about reached its credit limit.

The Democrats' Flawed Response

Due to the Democrats incorrectly assessing today's predicament, their attempts at getting things back on track are marginally successful at best. They're a bit like a family with an unemployed head of the household and a college age son who can't find a summer job. Just as they are pondering the poor job market, they wake up to the fact that their house desperately needs a fresh coat of paint. When they put the two realities together, it only seems logical to go to the bank, take out a home equity loan and hire their teenager to do the painting. This way the son gets a summer job and money for school and the house gets a much needed facelift.

On the surface this may appear prudent, but it really only worsens their plight. For the son's increase in income is one and the same as the family's increase in indebtedness. In fact, it is even worse than a simple transfer of funds from one pocket to another. For the family is now not only out the money they have paid their son, they also have to pay back the interest on the bank loan, bear the cost of the paint and pay higher interest rates on future loans. That is, if they can obtain them, as this increased debt load makes them a riskier loan prospect.

What the family needs is real income from an outside source. An example of this, using our illustration again, would be the son getting a job producing something. Then the money in his pocket would be coming from someplace other than the family's own checking account. In so doing, he'd actually participate in the laws of supply and demand. He'd be providing something (supply) to meet the needs of a customer (demand) who is able to pay for it. This results in wealth accumulation for the family.

The Republicans' Flawed Response

When Republicans pull their heads out of the same hole we've all dug together, they come up with a completely different and equally impoverishing idea for solving it. As strict believers in free markets, they'd have us go toe-to-toe with the third world countries that now compete for the jobs we sent overseas.

They look around and see that many competing countries don't have a minimum wage, so they attempt to freeze increases on ours or do away with it altogether. They also notice other nations cut costs by ignoring pollution and safety standards that we take for granted in the US. Again, out of a desire to be competitive, they seek to relax or do away with regulations we have in place here.

The question is, do we really want to do whatever it takes to compete with populations that have no labor laws, no safety or environmental standards and would be thrilled to earn a mere $700 a year? If we do win, at what cost do we win? Under these circumstances, is not winning the same as surrendering the high standard of living our parents and grandparents fought so hard to create? We're already seeing that for many, the minimum wage has become the maximum wage, and what was once a rock bottom floor has become a new ceiling. Americans now have to work longer and harder, not at one, but two or three jobs just to pay the same bills that one paycheck used to cover. As time moves on, fewer and fewer good jobs are available anywhere for anyone. It's not just the assembly line worker who is out of work, now it's also the car dealer and cabinet maker who no longer have the funds to be cash paying customers themselves as they no longer have the assembly line workers to purchase their goods. It's the police officers and school teachers in municipalities who no longer have the tax revenues to support them, and church pastors and chaplains, like me, who find church budgets shrinking.

Please Note: Just as one good rain is not the end of a drought, so, too, even if there is an economic upswing, it doesn't change the fact that America is hemorrhaging money.

New World Order Created by Republicans and Democrats

Each proposed response to our already bleak economy, from both the Democrats and Republicans, is scary enough when taken individually, but when put together, we have the true horror that is unfolding right before our very eyes. When adjusted for inflation, we are actually earning far less than our parents did (thanks to the Republican disdain for both collective bargaining and hiking the minimum wage). Then, to cover the shortfall that is created when lower wages bring in reduced tax revenues, we borrow more and more from China, the very nation that has us by the throat.

Put the two together and the Republicans have us work harder for less income and the Democrats borrowing more to make up the difference. One feeds into the other and worsens the whole. The longer this goes on and the deeper we sink, the better it is for China. For we are no longer merely consumers of their goods. They use the profit they make from us to loan us the money we need in order to cover the shortfall of revenue we're losing to them. We're increasingly like coal miners shopping at the company store. The question is, "At what point will we no longer be able to fund the interest on the debt, let alone pay off the principle?"

Enter the Wisdom of Roe Nelson

This whole mess could have been avoided if we all grew up, as I did, across the street from the Nelsons on Colston Drive in Chevy Chase, Maryland. They were faithful members of St. Paul Methodist Church where my father was the pastor.

When I was an enterprising young man of eleven, I walked across the street and asked Mrs. Nelson if I could mow her lawn. My sales pitch was simple. I'd cut the whole thing, the front and back yard, for only 50 cents. The words were barely out of my mouth before she replied, "Yeah, but what about David? He has a family to feed?"

With that my heart sank, not because I didn't get the job, but because I immediately knew, even at the age of eleven, that I had missed the mark and failed morally. She was right. What about David? David was the swellest guy (eleven year old terminology) I'd ever met. He was a kind, elderly man who drove his rickety truck out to the burbs every week only to have us kids swear, in all sincerity, that our dogs would never bite him despite the fact that they never stopped nipping at his heels.

David didn't merely mow lawns, he manicured them. He worked and worked, trimmed and trimmed until every three bedroom home looked like a regal estate. He earned a lot more than the $6.00 he charged the Nelsons (good money in 1966 dollars.) He earned the highest respect of everyone he met. I'd only be too proud to become a man like David. The question remains, "What about David?" He had expenses beyond my nickel ice cream cones and 50 cent movie tickets. He had a wife, probably house payments and grand-kids. While I'd be thrilled to live on a mere fraction of his paycheck, there was no way in the world that he could lower his rates sufficiently to compete with me.

If we translate this to global economics, we'd easily equate American workers today with David. They didn't just happen upon their standard of living, they earned it. On the basis of their efforts, they have assumed lifelong responsibilities they can't and shouldn't easily put aside. To pull the rug out from under them by handing their livelihoods over to people living in a totally foreign economy that requires infinitely less and to do it all in the name of "fair" trade is an assault on everything I know to be good and decent and true. Yet it is exactly what has happened to Davids all over this great country.

Can We Get It For Less?

In the late 1990s, I was a pastor who met with a committee responsible for hiring a new church secretary. We had managed to find the perfect candidate, a woman who is still there to this day. To my amazement and deep dissatisfaction, the question the panel asked wasn't, "What's the most we can offer her?" Rather, it was, "What's the least we can offer without losing her?" This was a church committee! I was so beside myself that when we finally did hire her, I immediately sought her out, apologized for the pittance we were paying and told her that henceforth this congregation wouldn't be singing *They Will Know We Are Christians By Our Love* until the church earned the right to do so.

When It Comes to Economics
The Circle Will Truly Be Unbroken!

What am I missing here? This a democratic country where each time we offer to employ someone, be it a babysitter or corporate executive, we have the right to be either good, loving and decent, or we can selfishly nickel and dime each person like a bunch of Ebenezer Scrooges. The economy will continue either way, but I offer all of us this fair warning. When it comes to finances, the circle will definitely be unbroken. The same tide that goes out eventually comes back in. There are no supernatural, beyond our control, don't know what we can do about it, mysterious "market forces at work" here. It's only us. We are the ones who hire, fire and set the wages.

Sooner or later, the amount we give out to others as employers will be the same feast or famine that is available when it is our turn to sit at the table. The dollars that leave our hands when we employ someone are the same dollars that are drawn upon when we ourselves seek a fair, livable wage as a worker. Put a lot in and get a lot out. Put in a morsel, and we'll all barely scrape by like dogs under their master's table. We can create a nation of well-paying jobs, or we can continue to take on the role of paupers. It's up to us, for ultimately, we are in fact our "brother's keeper."

Of Fire and Water

I'd like to offer a few brief observations about money. First, the scout in me tells me building a sound economy is best likened to building a roaring fire. When good, honorable wages are given in exchange for good, honorable work, it is akin to putting logs at the base. For the working class, unlike the wealthy, cannot afford to sideline their money. They spend it almost as quickly as it comes in. This provides a constant source of fuel that heats up the entire economy from the bottom to the top.

The other image that comes to mind is water. Water, by nature, naturally flows to the lowest point available. When a fabulously wealthy economy at the top of its game is put right next to the poorest economy at the bottom (for that's where the US and China were in 1972), and all of the barriers between them are removed, it's only obvious and natural that two things are going to happen. First, the levels in China are going to rise and levels in America are going to fall. How could it be any other way? And, that is exactly what has happened. It only seems equally obvious to me that while we still have some water in our pool, we'd better stem the tide.

What about Wages and Inflation?

Having gone through years of self-inflicted poverty out of a deep seated desire to lend assistance to others, I know firsthand about "huffing it down the road" with only shoe leather to soften, if not the ride, then definitely the stride. While a marked improvement over going barefoot, shoe leather had its limitations. And so, in time, all that wishful thinking by many a walker about floating down the road on a cushion of air led to someone coming up with the idea of an inflatable tire. What's significant here is that a tire is, in a sense, a closed system or universe. It has to be this way in order to hold enough air together in a compressed state so as to raise it up to a new level, a level above the rest, a level that is so wonderful it is not only like, but actually is floating on air.

Now, Lord knows there is plenty of air outside the tire. It's all around, infinitely cheap and instantly available, but pity the fool that opens the valve trying to take advantage of it. All that happens is that the tire loses pressure and the whole thing goes flat, leaving one stranded as others race past.

I Fear We Are Like That Fool

Of course, wages are going to be lower outside our borders, in countries that are impoverished, but trying to take advantage of them is as foolish as trying to replace pressurized air with unpressurized air. It, too, will leave us deflated and parked by the curb. Right now, our tires are riding awfully low and we need to pump them up again. To do so is really quite simple. It's a two-step process. First, we need to apply patches where needed and seal up any leaks, and then pump up our standard of living by allowing wages to return to the levels they were at before we opened the valves.

We Mustn't Hinder the Natural Increase of Wages

We have been told over and over again that inflation is bad, that the government must stop it cold in its tracks whenever and wherever it rears its ugly head. The question is, where are these opportunities? We are led to believe that nothing can be done about the dramatic upswing in the cost OPEC charges for oil, even though they know they can always depend on us to send in troops to do their bidding when they get into trouble; and these wars aren't cheap. They drive inflation right through the roof.

We also know that drug companies, even those based in the US, get away with charging us more than anyone else in the world for the very medications they manufacture here. Why? It is simply because they can. In fact, Uncle Sam has flat out rejected using its position as the nation's largest health care consumer to negotiate lower drug costs on our behalf. And the list goes on and on and on. In fact, I can't think of too many prices or charges the government regulates, except for public utilities.

But when it is our turn to seek increases in our pay checks so that we might maintain buoyancy with these rising costs that threaten to drown us in red ink, watch out! Would-be watchdogs in Congress, who take pride in protecting us from rising inflation, jump up and pounce. "Inflationary," they cry as they rush in to freeze increases in our personal incomes.

When I was coming up in the 1950's and 60's, costs were going up, but wages were keeping pace with them. Inflation was there, but like grace that can always stretch just a little bit more to cover increases in sin, wages somehow always rose with them and we were OK. All of that changed when Ronald Reagan became President. The minimum wage became frozen and remained that way for years.

Now, in fairness to him, it is true that he entered office in a time of outrageous inflation and the brakes had to be put on whenever possible, but the problem was that those brakes were never released once the economy improved. From then on, other forms of wealth accumulation were allowed to increase, but wage increases were automatically deemed "inflationary" and curtailed.

We want to slow increases in everything except wages. For when costs remain the same and wages increase, our standard of living goes up…Think about it!

Where Was Our Government When We As Workers Needed Protection?

The problem is, Administration after Administration have sat by and passively watched as foreign companies, with the active support of their home governments, have practiced every trick in the book to gain market share. For the folks in Washington to be all laissez-faire fare and hands off while American workers were getting clobbered by these conspiratorial trade practices and then turn around and be on us like syrup on pancakes the few times we were able to catch a break and get a raise is the height of hypocrisy. It seems folks in Washington have forgotten that it is government "For the People."

The One-Two Punch to the American Standard of Living

The first blow came when Ronald Reagan did battle with unions that were a bit too greedy for their own good. Air traffic controllers went on strike and when they didn't meet his deadline for returning to work, they were summarily fired. Subsequent unions fell one by one, including Greyhound bus drivers who watched in horror as a fellow worker got run over by one of their own buses and subsequently died. This was soon followed by the squashing of any and all attempts to raise the minimum wage.

The second blow came from the Bushes' and Clintons' push for globalization. First, there was George Bush I's relentless call for a "New World Order" followed by Bill Clinton's push for the North American Free Trade Agreement (NAFTA). Together, they put downward pressure on wages as they expanded the pool of workers to include the entire globe. Whereas before Americans were only competing against each other for work, now, all of a sudden, they found themselves competing with workers around the world who could live on substantially less money in foreign countries.

From that point on, American workers didn't stand a chance. They had it coming from above and below. On the top side, they found it hard to get any increases in pay as the unions that kept pushing for higher and higher wages with better and better benefits were suddenly gone. On the low side, globalization meant employers could now reach across the oceans and get the same work done for a fraction of what they were previously paying workers here. The American Dream of making it big financially was now severely crippled and our lives have been forever changed.

The Difference Between Now and Then

A century earlier, the great robber barons of the Gilded Age, the likes of the Rockefellers and Carnegies, had also benefitted from cheap labor. They, too, had made their millions off of the backbreaking sweat of others. That wasn't new. It's as old as capitalism itself. The tradeoff back then was that even though the workers of that day didn't reap the full rewards to which they were entitled, their future descendants did. That was about to change.

What was new this time around was that American capitalists were no longer investing in America, but rather diverting funds from here to the industrialization and development of competing nations. It was no longer true that "What was good for GM was good for America." To the contrary, the exact opposite was often the case.

Undeterred, when we as consumers wanted more, we didn't look for raises. Rather, we kept going back again and again and breached the walls of our purposefully inflated, self-contained little economic bubble that we had been living in. This led to deflating our economic situation here while at the same time adding lift to competing economies.

Wages, like tires, do need to be inflated from time to time. It's true. Just try to drive a car or an economy where that hasn't been done in a few years and you'll know what I'm talking about.

A Long String of Presidents Have Presided Over the Great American Giveaway

All kinds of Presidential libraries can be built and all manner of foundations started to honor the memory of our eight past heads of state, but no amount of window dressing can cover the simple fact that this country has been in a persistent state of decline for decades. The facts speak for themselves.

On the watch of President after President, from both sides of the aisle, the United States has stumbled and stumbled badly. It has lost ground, thereby opening the door for lesser countries to rush in and gain political, economic, and industrial clout.

The ineptitude of these "leaders" has been striking. How else can we explain going from a safe cruising altitude to a precipitous nosedive in little more than a single generation? Opportunity after opportunity has been squandered time and time again. These lapses in judgment have been so severe that the common citizen cannot help but wonder just who side these "leaders" has been on. Did they actually think extending "most favored nation status" to another country meant favoring their interests above ours? Judging from their track record, it would seem they actually did, for in situation after situation, their decisions increased the standing of other nations while diminishing ours.

Let's be clear. The "Great American Giveaway" didn't start with China. It started much earlier than that with Japan. China has merely been following their playbook. Both countries lured us in with their cheap labor only to then systematically begin to take, take, take and take some more. They smiled and bowed to us as they toured our jet propulsion laboratories and manufacturing plants (all the while taking copious notes).

They studied at our best universities and made detailed blueprints of our most innovative products, then went home and set up state of the art factories to compete against us. And where were our nation's leaders? They were busy smiling and bowing right back at them.

Which President stood up when Japan dumped artificially cheap steal on Bethlehem, Pennsylvania, wiping out a proud industry and pillar of American strength? Not one of them.

Which President took decisive action when the Japanese government repeatedly usurped the concept of fair trade by actively doing whatever it took to defeat American competition one industry at a time? Again, not one of them rose to our defense. Reagan finally did step in to protect Harley Davidson, but that was the only company. The rest of our manufacturers were on their own, and as a result, a large number of them no longer exist or are greatly diminished.

President after President made sure we kept on the straight and narrow and played by the rules while at the same time doing nothing to stem the illicit practices aimed at our workers and the nation as a whole. This dynamic was reminiscent of US Olympic Teams competing before the fall of the communist bloc. Back then, our athletes, with little or no financial support, went up against East Germans who had been in government funded sports camps since childhood. To sweeten the deal even further, their coaches stepped in and doled out huge amounts of performance enhancing drugs and hormones so potent as to call into question the very gender of their female athletes.

When the Japanese took all of the money they had accrued from years of lopsided trading and set out to buy America, what Administration so much as raised a protest let alone acted to stop it? Not one of them. If it wasn't for a protracted slump in their economy, the Japanese would probably own enormous chunks of America by now including much of Manhattan just as they currently own much of Hawaii. So easily we forget that Reagan's first trip after leaving office was to fly directly to Japan to receive a check for 2 million dollars. What was the rationale for Japan paying him so much money?

It was supposedly for delivering a few speeches. Delivering a few speeches? Do the math. Ronald Reagan earned $400,000 a year. To earn $2,000,000 he would have had to work for five years as chief executive or "deliver a few speeches" in Japan so insignificant that none of us know hardly anything about them.

Look at the Japanese industrial market share before he took office and compare it to where it was after he left office. Then look at what happened to America's factories and our workforce during the same period. I'd say that Japan got an incredible deal for a mere $2 million.

Which President took steps to protect our technology from blatant theft by our competitors? Not one of them. Which President took steps to keep wages of the American worker high? Barack Obama, almost single handedly saved Detroit's auto industry and with it what little remains of our industrial complex, but for the most part, Chief Executive after Chief Executive have sat idly by and watched our standard of living plummet.

To top it off, American companies are saddled with an ever increasing barrage of rules and regulations that tip the scales even more in their competitors' favor. America is now one of the last places in the world where one would want to open a factory. We can't even speak to an American sales rep when we dial up an American corporation as a huge percentage of customer call centers are now located overseas in places like the Philippines and other foreign lands.

Presently, we export more empty boxes than products and borrow bazillions and bazillions of dollars every year, not to pay the principle, mind you, but rather just the interest on our ever growing loan to China. Why, pray tell, do we even have unemployment claims of American workers who can't find jobs here while we are buying things from the very same China that turns around and collects interest on the money we are borrowing to support our idled work force. It is absolutely ludicrous.

We may have the largest Navy in the world, but so what? We don't even control the western hemisphere anymore. China does by virtue of it turning the Monroe Doctrine on its head by buying control of the canal from corrupt Panamanian officials. Bill Clinton did nothing to stop it. Why didn't he intervene? It's because he took campaign contributions from China and therefore was obliged to keep his mouth shut when it happened.

Since then, there hasn't been so much as a verbal rebuke of either Panama or China regarding the sale, let alone a change in China's most favored nation status. To the contrary, with the ongoing silence of each successive Presidential Administration, China has become so secure in its new found home away from home that it is now working to dramatically increase the size of ships that can pass through under their watchful eye, as we sit back and get accustomed to our new role as mere spectators. As if this isn't bad enough, that same nation is now embarking on construction of a second wider canal.

It is beyond even Webster's definition of "pathetic." Here we are with our national leadership, acting like a bunch of deer in the headlights, passively watching ships go through what in effect has become China's canal. Worse yet, many of you readers are probably wondering by now, "Why all of the focus on China?" The answer is really quite simple. It's because no one else is raising any alarms.

The Chinese are like the student who arrived late and unprepared, yet had the good fortune to be befriended by a classmate who allowed the copying of answers that were obtained by the first student studying long and hard into the night.

I'm quite certain that instead of focusing on the boost the US gave China, there will be a backlash of scorn once we stem the flow; for by continually giving with no expectation of anything in return, we've created a sense of entitlement that can only lead to resentment once the well beaten path of a one sided relationship is no longer used.

As it is, we've given them cause to believe that if they continue to manipulate their currency to their unfair trade advantage, ignore our copyright laws, allow the pervasive pirating of our name brands and introduce, on occasion, dangerous toxins into products we consume our only response will be to send over a polite delegation to have a little chat. Of course, these conversations have never changed anything due to the simple fact that the Chinese aren't stupid.

Something tells me they aren't exactly trembling in their boots. They know that if they continue to ignore us, the worse that will happen is that we will send over yet another delegation with the fair warning that if things don't turn around quickly, we'll be back to speak with them yet again.

What Shall I Say To Those Who Have Gone On Before?

Those of you who are so casual and nonplused about surrendering our position of prominence, not to just any nation, but to one that has gobbled down whatever has been handed to them on a silver platter and stolen the rest...please tell me, what should I say to those who have gone before us when we meet on some ethereal shore and they inquire as to their beloved country? Should I tell them, who gave even when they had nothing left to give, that we just got bored with the blessings and opted to give them away? Is that what I should tell them?

And what, pray tell, should I say to the legions of brave souls, the likes of John Paul Jones, who, when asked if he was going to surrender, replied, "I have not yet begun to fight!" or to the farm boys of Pennsylvania and Delaware whose frozen feet bled in the snow at Valley Forge? Do I tell them that we felt it was inevitable that another country would overtake us and, therefore, put up not the slightest resistance?

And what, may I ask, do I say to those whose bodies are still trapped beneath the decks of the Battleship

Arizona or are buried in Flanders Fields when they ask about their nation and its place in the world? Do I tell them that we surrendered it to not just any nation, but to a nation that kills prisoners in order to sell their organs to the highest bidder and forces couples who conceive more than one child to have an abortion even if it is against their will? Is that the message you want to give these brave builders of our republic? That we just assumed our time was over because the television commentators kept saying over and over again that all empires rise only to fall and our time had run its course? No, I won't be telling them any such thing. You'll have to share the news. For I have neither the heart nor the stomach to convey such sadness.

Hello?
Where In The World
Have Our "Leaders" Been?
What Have They Been Doing?

Name the government official, from any party or branch of our government, who has raised holy havoc over China's repeated attempts at hacking into our national security computers. There aren't any such voices, at least at high enough levels of power to be heard, that have stood up and said, "Stop!" Name the official, from either party, who has told China that Antarctica belongs to everyone, so come back, pick up the flag you planted on the bottom of the ocean floor and please don't upset the tranquility of the place by trying another stunt like that again. Name the American President, Republican or Democrat, who has stood up to China's clear acts of aggression and called a spade a spade. There aren't any. Why not?

China Has Been Waging
A Cyber and/or Trade War
And We Respond As If
To An Isolated Crime Here And There.
Why?

To classify these provocative actions as mere "cybercrimes" is a gross mischaracterization of the seriousness of these aggressive acts. To under respond only encourages more incursions as it conveys weakness or worse yet, a total indifference on our part.

No One in Washington Seems Too Awfully Concerned

For over forty years, we have extended China our "most favored nation" trade status and put up with their trade policies that are clearly designed to siphon wealth from our nation and send it to theirs. Yet, no one has put up the warning flags let alone called for action. To the contrary, Administration after Administration, from Nixon to the present, have bent over backwards to accommodate China's gorilla-like trade practices that have robbed us blind, while at the same time, holding budget talks on cutting services here at home.

Globalization Leads to Individual Disempowerment

While it may feel wise to bring all of the world's people under one global umbrella as the larger the political entity the fewer the borders that foster conflict and division, in reality, it diminishes the goal of equal representation. For the larger the crowd, the harder it is to have individual voices heard and the more tempting it is for power mongers to seek dominance. Democracies function best when people have a sense of ownership and rightfully believe that their individual input matters.

That is why we have municipal and county governments, then state governments, and finally the national or federal government. If we want to change something on the local level, we, as individuals, can deal with it on the local level where a lone voice is most powerful. The larger the issue, the more people are needed to bring attention to it. In this way, the system retains proportionality. One person can be heard on things that affect him or her directly, but they need the support of the masses to affect change on issues that impact the whole.

To keep our country spinning like a top
we must remember:

It Can
Be Rightfully
Said That Democracies
Are At Their Strongest When
Individuals Feel They Are
Not only Encouraged,
But Obliged to
Participate
As Their
Voices
Really
Do
Count.
Conversely,
They Are Weakest
When Their Citizens Succumb to
Feeling that They Are Powerless, Insignificant,
Even Irrelevant, When They Are Led to Believe Nothing
They Do Will Have Any Impact on the Powers That Be, For
They Are Outsiders Who Are Only Able to Look In, That The
Truth of the Matter is Governmental Structures are Mere
Window Dressings Designed to Create the Illusion of Power
When, in Truth People Are but as Tiny Leaves Caught up &
Swept Downstream in the Mighty Torrent Of History. And
Since There Isn't Anything We Can Do To Change
This, Why Bother Even Getting Involved?
To Refute This Lie, the Ongoing Challenge
Of Any Democracy Is To Protect It
From Those Who Would
Manipulate The
System For
Their Own
Selfish
Goals

Lions and Tigers and Bears, Oh My!

Even Dorothy knew who to fear; why don't we? In 1982, when Ronald Reagan borrowed a line from Leon Trotsky's 1917 speech and spoke of communism taking its rightful place on the "ash heap of history," we as a people celebrated victory in the Cold War and put communism and the fear of communists behind us. We bid it adieu and considered it to be little more than a spooky villain in the dust of our rear view mirror; but, was it really over? As fate would have it, just as we lassoed the mighty Russian Bear of Soviet era communism, we saw out of the corner of our eye a little, cute, cuddly Chinese Tiger cub that we couldn't resist picking up. The rest is playing out the way it so often does for owners of exotic animals. The once cute and innocent grows over time into the aggressive animal it was destined to become. Before those who adopted it can adjust, the nature of the relationship turns and the cute little cub becomes a four hundred pound killer.

How Russian Bears and Chinese Tigers Differ

Yes, it is true that we put that big old Russian Bear in its place, but as contests go, that wasn't anything compared to the potential challenge before us. While bears, by nature, are large and ferocious, they are also terribly awkward and clumsy. They have an unsteady gait and often roll over when attempting to sit up straight. They get pudgy and bloated with fat from laziness (just look at Winnie the Pooh), while tigers, on the other hand, are sleek and immaculately clean.

Tigers move silently through the forest, surefooted and careful to slouch down, waiting for the opportune moment to strike. They have no need to show forth their intentions or demonstrate force, for they are the consummate hunters. They know the value of sitting motionless, biding their time, waiting with uncommon focus for just the right moment to pounce. While bears often take on other bears in a demonstration of their strength, tigers have no need for such displays of force. They rarely make a premature stand, show their teeth or raise their voices. They prefer to sit quietly by and wait and wait for the perfect opportunity to strike. There is a reason most will hunt bears and avoid tigers.

I had a cat when I had a basement apartment in New York City. My home was in the back of the building, immediately next to the laundry room and the trash room, a true Shangri La for the urban mouse. I had often heard that New York had more rodents than people, but never thought too much about it until I got this cat. I also had a dog. He was into everything and then some, but not this cat. It just sat there hour after hour, day after day, staring at the baseboard.

Many a morning, I'd come out of my room and there would be the kill from the night before. There never was any chance of the cat losing the fight, just a dead mouse, lying lifeless on the carpet. Though only a house cat, and a declawed one at that, I learned that a cat, any size cat, never looks very threatening. They don't bark like a dog or prowl around like a bear. In fact, they appear totally disinterested as they lounge around preening themselves, looking totally non-threatening.

Many a wildebeest or zebra come to the water for a drink. They see the mighty tiger sitting on the rock as he normally does, enjoying the sun. This day, the tiger appears no more antagonistic than on any of the countless days before. Concerned, but thirsty, the unsuspecting victim bends his neck forward for a drink, a nice cool drink of refreshing water. Then, without notice, the tiger is suddenly upon him. There's never any question as to who will win for the tiger knows the value of biding his time. Day after day, he just sat there, totally at ease, until his prey became whittled down to complete complacency. Then, when everything was in the cat's favor, the attack occurred. There was no real competition to speak of, only a futile last ditch effort at defense, but never really a contest. It was too late for that. The patient tiger had carefully scoped out the situation and as a result, emerged once more victorious.

Please, Do Not Feed the Tiger

I want to be clear. I harbor no ill will toward the people of China. It is only the pernicious leadership that I fault. Indeed, I am a bit like those who admire tigers at the zoo, ever mindful that less than 1% of the total animal is problematic with its killer instinct. If that wasn't present, my home and my yard would be full of the beautiful creatures. Yet, that isn't the case. It is only because all of the rest of the animal is subject to and responsive to the directing of the head that I have no choice but to keep my distance and respect the sign saying, "Please, Do Not Feed the Tiger."

How It Will All Go Down If We Don't Now Rise Up

What we need to come to terms with is the simple fact that the fall of nations is like the collapse of companies. In an effort to hold onto the confidence of all involved, companies will go to great lengths to hide their financial woes lest stocks and credit ratings plummet. Things look as normal as they can possibly make them right up until the last moment. Then, one fine morning, the plug is pulled and the whole thing collapses like an inflatable building that has just shut off the fans.

We Are In an Epic Struggle
Of
Freedom vs.
Tyranny
~ If Only We Could
Accept It ~

Clearly, It's Time to Talk about China

Nations the world over have consistently been able to turn to the United States, the birthplace of modern democracy, whenever their most basic human freedoms have been threatened. We have been the global power that has fought back and curtailed the authoritarian rule of the Hitlers, Mussolinis, Mao's, Stalins and Khrushchevs of the world. To now let down our guard and slowly, but oh, so steadily, hand over the role of dominant global power to a communist country that forbids the distribution of Bibles and routinely tramples the most basic of human rights just so we can profit off their cheap labor is the height of moral failures.

The Real Battlefield Is Ultimately Economic

We think we are safe because of our enormous military, but this is misguided. The truth of the matter is regardless of its size, it can't save us if we don't have the capital necessary to hold it up. The Soviet Union was strong right up to the last minute. Then, in the blinking of an eye, their economy collapsed. Almost immediately thereafter, their military unraveled and their once proud fleet of nuclear submarines and surface ships, which until recently patrolled much of the earth, suddenly lay abandoned, rusting in Soviet ports. When there are calls for enlarging our current global military presence to stand up to the growing threat of China, it is clear that Washington doesn't get it. We can't maintain a global military presence without the income to support it.

China understands this. That is why, learning from the mistakes of the Soviet Union, they have put the actual arming of the country last and instead have focused all of their efforts on first growing strong as a nation. Once this threshold is met, watch out. Their militarization will be fast and furious and will come just about the time the US will be too depleted, too gaunt, and financially anemic to respond.

Unlike the former Soviet Union where they were always on the field militarily, always advancing here and there, the Chinese are like the prize fighter who knows the very last thing a contender does is put on the gloves. This has lured us into believing we have nothing at all to worry about. So, we keep diverting our wealth to them by shopping at Wal-Mart while they are busy using this money to condition themselves and get into shape. Once they feel fully prepared to take us on, then, God forbid, we will be like the 90 pound weakling trying to defend ourselves against the ultimate of muscular opponents.

Excuse me for a moment.
I need to make a phone call ...

"Hello, National Archives?
Dig up Paul Revere's horse..."

The Chinese
Are Coming!

I'd Argue That Time
Is of The Essence

It is simply beyond my capacity to fathom the fact that to date no one on Capitol Hill has even mentioned the possibility of standing up to the Chinese. Isn't it obvious that if we continue down our current path of business as usual, in another four years chances are good that two things will have taken place? First, as mentioned, China will have siphoned enough wealth that we won't have any consumer strength left. It will all be in their pockets. This feeds into the second probability that this money will then go into China's military industrial complex, and we will be forced to spend whatever we have left on defense. That, however, will be a losing proposition as without any real tangible income from industry, we will only have the option to borrow. The problem, of course, is that we cannot borrow from Europe as they, too, are in the soup with us. The only nation with the capital to lend us money will be China, and I tend to doubt that they will be willing to fund our military defense.

Import Duties Aimed Specifically at China Are Our Only Hope

They will immediately bring our jobs back home, erase our trade deficit, restore our local, state and federal treasuries and deflate China's growing military threat before it is too late. We need to immediately place, across the board, graduated duties on all Chinese imports. Our goal is not to inflict damage on China. We need to be real clear about that. Rather, it is purely defensive; to protect ourselves from the unfair trade policies they have had in place for decades.

Few would argue that when someone is playing dirty, it is not only right, but morally responsible to take protective measures to defend against unfair assault. In light of this basic human right of self-preservation, the gradual but real introduction of import duties is warranted. I'd suggest a 25% increase per year for four consecutive years until we reach the level we have in mind. Quite simply, I am suggesting that we do this to bring home the very factories that have impoverished us with their departure and made China rich. It's as simple as that, for factories produce goods, and it is the sale of these goods that creates wealth.

Cut off the economic incentives to manufacture goods over there and in short order we will once again start producing our own consumer goods right here at home. Even if we lose trade with them, we are better off without it as they have tilted the whole equation in their favor. For the entire thing has been set up to drain the lifeblood out of our nation, and we are all suffering a dramatic loss in our standard of living because of it. Figure it out. It's not that complicated.

"But, We Don't Want To Set Off A Trade War!"

I hate to be the bearer of bad news, but anytime you live in a country where consumers are hard pressed to find any, and I repeat, *any* domestically made products, where virtually all of the merchandise on the store shelves have a "made somewhere else" label on them, there is little chance of an impending trade war. Why? Because it has already come and gone, and you've undoubtedly lost!

Let me tell you something else. . . the only thing more humiliating than being the wealthiest power on earth to lose to what started out as the poorest is to have a government so inept that it virtually slept right through it. Now that's humiliating. And yet, these same "leaders" have no shame. They now seek our vote to return them to office. Are they serious?! To now stir up fear among us over a potential trade war with China is like advising the Confederacy not to get on the wrong side of the North after Sherman returns from burning Atlanta.

Damn it!
We Shouldn't Have To Support
Communism Every Time We Shop.

Congress: Get busy and pass legislation aimed at restoring the very jobs that were rightfully here and never should have left our shores in the first place. Until this step is taken, our wealth will keep flowing overseas.

Quite simply, we need to listen to our vocabulary, to the words that flow from our lips. For there is indeed a reason we refer to factories as "plants." They, too, are like a farmer's field that takes the rawest of materials and blends them together in a unique and wonderful way so as to produce something entirely new that others crave and are willing to purchase. It's true. Just as a farm takes the raw materials of soil, sunlight, seed, water and air to create food, so, too, manufacturing plants take metals, glass, rubber and synthetics to create a whole host of products from automobiles and toaster ovens to electronics.

So quickly we forget that the American Revolution was fought over the right to manufacture.

Why? Why was the right to have our own factories so important? It is because our founding fathers realized something we have somehow forgotten, namely that the ground floor of economic prosperity is production. It is only after we create wealth by bringing to the table something entirely new that didn't exist before that we have something to trade. That position of affluence stays with us until we spend it down and have to go out and produce more. Like people, when nations sell stuff, they gain wealth and when they buy stuff they lose wealth.

An Economy is Like a Farm

In the final analysis, it doesn't matter or make the slightest bit of difference how many hours a farmer works or how nice the place looks. The barns can be nice and tidy, freshly painted and immaculately maintained. The tractors can be kept in tip-top shape, the fences mended and the house without blemish, yet none of this determines the health of the farm. All that matters is the size of the crop.

It's just that simple. That is why creating the "busy work" of paving roads and planting trees doesn't offset the money we are sending China every time we shop. They are the ones producing things and we are not. Instead, we are buying what they produce. Then, as if to add insult to injury, we are borrowing from them to prop up the economy we decimated by exporting our industrial base to them.

How You Know if Your Hometown and/or Country is in Trouble

Take a look around. Don't be fooled by employment numbers, for employment numbers alone can be misleading. A lot of people can be working, but if their labors are not in production, then you are not in a prosperous community. This simple point is something a huge number of politicians, and I dare say economists, don't get, but that's O.K. Sometimes it is up to simpletons like us to point out the obvious to those who we'd hope would know better, but unfortunately don't.

Now, hang in there with me and let's see if we can turn this thing around. O.K., by definition, prosperity is about increase and increase is about creating things that did not exist before. When we write a new song or grow a new crop or produce a new manufactured item that is of value to others and can be sold to others, then we are moving forward or "getting ahead." That's wonderful.

What we don't want is to be in an economic situation like the one I currently see in my community and perhaps the one you see in yours. All of the manufacturing jobs are gone. *Poof* they've disappeared. In their place there have sprung up all kinds of resale shops. In a town of roughly 30,000 people, there are now between 10 to 12 secondhand resale stores. It's pitiful. The once great economic powerhouse, the mighty United States of America, is no longer forging ahead, but now is sitting there, dead in the water, idle. Not only aren't we producing anything, we're just standing still like a cow chewing its cud, reprocessing that which we have already consumed. Increasingly, the only new products on the shelves are made overseas. My God! What has happened to the once proud, robust country I grew up in?

Why not have a 20% rise in employment instead of the measly 1 or 2% we now experience?

It's just as easy as it is ethical to accomplish. Just replace the "Made in China" labels with our old "Made in America" labels and we'll enjoy the same prosperity that was ours before our elected officials and selfish business executives opted to give it away to a nation that is using and will continue to use the proceeds to fund our demise.

The same production jobs that made China's economy soar can be ours once again by simply re-creating an environment where it makes good economic sense for Americans to manufacture the products that we Americans consume.

With a simple vote in Congress and stroke of the Presidential pen, we can make it more attractive to produce our own goods right here at home by putting import duties on Chinese goods. This will make Chinese goods more expensive than the goods made here in the USA, thus returning to us the home turf advantage. It will also level the playing field so as to offset four decades of China's artificially manipulating the whole equation in their favor.

*If the people with whom I did business
were shoplifting while they were billing me,
you'd better believe I wouldn't
just cut them a check.*

No, of course not! I'd call the police and make darn sure there were some serious consequences for the theft. I would then calculate the cost of what was stolen and deduct it from the bill. If we did just that and included not only the cost of what was stolen from our government such as defense technologies, but also all of the cost due to American companies from theft of their intellectual property, loss of royalties and the loss of sales from boatloads upon boatloads upon boatloads of shipping containers filled with pirated materials (while this anemic government sat by and did absolutely nothing to stop it), then added penalties and interest (hey, the IRS and Courts do it all of the time), I think that supposed debt we owe them could be reduced to practically nothing. In fact, they might be the ones owing us.

Renegotiate Our Supposed Debt Already!

Each one of the advanced systems they got from us came at enormous cost to taxpayers. How many launches, for example, did it take to put a man on the moon and return him safely to Earth? I'll tell you. It took all of the Mercury, Gemini and then Apollo missions and before that there were years of test flights by pilots such as Chuck Yeager who laid the groundwork for rocketry.

Now, thanks to us, the Chinese will apply all of that research and experimentation to build their first and only spaceship. It will undoubtedly reach the Moon on their first try, thanks to all they got from our years of development. Then they, like the Japanese before them with the transistor, will claim all of the glory and use that knowledge in direct competition with us. Renegotiate our supposed debt already! To go from rice paddies to space in 40 years is utterly impossible. We owe them? Yeah, right, sure we do!

America's Dunkirk

If we had some real leadership in Washington, we'd recognize that there's all kinds of capital lying around. I believe people would love to extend it to us, with interest, if it was explained to them that it is an issue of national importance; that we have to change course now and in order to do this, we have to keep things going at home in the meantime. OK, that's an easy sale. Most Americans are already there in their thinking. All we have to do is explain how they can help.

I'd either instigate new financial vehicles or reinvigorate existing ones such as US Savings Bonds and enlist celebrities and other folks to encourage people to invest. I'd make the interest rates quite generous, non-transferable and available only to American citizens. I'd also make the payoff years down the road as has always been the practice with Savings Bonds. Do this, and we'll have people take to their savings like the British to their boats when they saved their troops at Dunkirk.

This is infinitesimally less expensive than borrowing from a foreign nation that has made it abundantly clear that any money coming to them from us will be used to fund a government hell bent on doing us wrong. For in the latter case, we not only have to repay the debt, we also have to fund additional defensive measures we will have to take to protect us from the monster we are creating.

Why Are We Funding Another Evil Empire?

While we're at it, I think it worthwhile to discuss having a Constitutional Amendment prohibiting the sale of Treasury Bills to foreign nations lest we get into this vulnerable position ever again. It is bad enough that we have allowed ourselves to become indebted, but to know that a sizeable chunk of our GNP goes directly into funding a military industrial complex out to harm us is absurd.

Then There Is Europe

Our allies in Europe and their currency, the Euro, are on the brink of financial collapse. Import duties on Chinese goods will have the additional benefit of supporting these democracies who now find themselves in desperate straits with massive unemployment, in large part, because of our trade policies that have reached beyond our borders to impact their economies as well.

The fix is not sending more aid to these countries nor is it printing more US currency to do so. The solution is to immediately pass significant trade legislation that will make it just as unattractive to produce goods in communist China as it is attractive to produce them right here in the democratic United States and democratic Europe.

Upset The Chinese?
They Hold Our Treasury Bills!

As newcomers to capitalism, China needs to know the other side of the equation. Firstly, there is some truth to the old adage that if a person owes the bank $1,000, the bank owns them, but if a person owes the bank $10,000,000, then they own the bank. They also need to know that there are no debtor's prisons in capitalism and declaring bankruptcy, while never easy, is always an option. Just because something is owed doesn't mean it should be repaid, especially if the lender is going to use the proceeds to harm the borrower. This truth applies to nations as well as neighbors.

Think about it, if England in the 1930's owed Germany billions of dollars prior to the outbreak of hostilities, do you think they'd be rushing to repay it? Of course, they wouldn't! If anything, they'd use their indebtedness as a bargaining chip to convince Germany to back away from its increasingly aggressive behaviors. Churchill was able to see the conflict in Europe long before his own people did. Likewise, Roosevelt was able to see danger long before the rest of America did. Both took steps to sound the alarm and prepare. Who in our national leadership is able to see the obvious and act?

The Only Reason
Not To Install Import Duties
Is Fear

When I share my proposal of starting graduated import duties against China, the overwhelming response I get is based on fear. What will they do? The fact is, China may have our promissory notes, but who has the power there? They are at the mercy of our good intentions to pay them off. History is replete with instances where well intentioned promises are never kept. History also tells us that decisions based on fear and desires to appease are by far the worst possible courses of action for a nation to take. If we are fearful of China's long term intentions, then we had better examine our fears now so can take preemptive steps to protect ourselves.

I am reminded of the wealthy couple (true story) who hired a skipper to handle their yacht. Their friends remembered that before the couple turned up missing, they had verbalized concerns about their new employee and often spoke of just how uncomfortable they felt whenever they were around him. Despite this, they lacked the inner strength and backbone to take control of the situation and fire him. Why? Because they feared what he might do if they upset him. Hoping things would improve if they didn't "rock the boat," they reluctantly went ahead and set sail on their long planned ocean voyage. Well, guess what? Neither they nor their yacht were ever seen again.

Shame on Us!
The Saddest Day
In American History

Some would consider the outbreak of the Civil War, the day we were viciously attacked at Pearl Harbor or the events of 911 as the saddest days in American history. I beg to differ. Tragic as they were, they were attacks brought to bear by others on the sovereignty of the United States. In time, each of those incursions was reversed and America emerged victorious with its core values.

No, none of them were the saddest day in American history. The saddest, in my estimation, occurred on the day that we, as the most powerful nation in the world, stood silently by and did absolutely nothing to prevent the horrific, ruthless slaughter of innocent civilians in Tiananmen Square. What was their crime? They were so audacious as to seek freedom of assembly, the right to vote and the right of self-determination. They looked to America to assist in their quest, even going so far as to erect a replica of the Statue of Liberty in their midst and we didn't so much as lift a finger to help. Nothing, nothing at all was done. No military threats were uttered, no troops repositioned, no sanctions taken. Why? It was because we didn't want to upset the Chinese communist regime and jeopardize the potential fortunes that American corporations were beginning to reap there.

On that day, America surrendered its soul. It sold it for a mess of pottage. Decades later, those who were not killed in the attack in Tiananmen Square still languish in China's prisons. Where's our sack cloth? Where are our ashes? Are the spirits within us so dead that even now we cannot even feel, let alone own, the shame that should confront and confound us?

With One Vote for Import Duties on China:

1) America will start to recover its industrial base.

2) We'll have the tax revenues for infrastructure.

3) The USA will become prosperous once again.

4) Parents will be home raising their kids instead of working two or more jobs just to pay the bills.

5) China will be forced to deal with internal pressures that will divert their resources away from its aggressive posturing.

CLEANING

UP

AFTER THE

PARTIES

The Great American
Tune-up

Feeling Invisible

Unlike newly formed democracies where people walk miles and miles in order to cast their vote and get that coveted splash of ink on their finger, we feel so powerless, so unable to be heard in this country that many of us have intentionally tuned out.

I see it all of the time. I ask people, particularly younger people, about what's going on out there in the world around them and find an astonishingly high percentage don't have the slightest clue. When I pepper them with questions, it becomes readily apparent that they don't read the paper or watch the news and neither do any of the people in their home. That sense of wanting, of needing to know because "I want to cast my vote or write my Congressman or fight for this or that cause" is all but completely gone.

This is what lobbyists, special interests, big money and pollsters that broadcast what people are thinking long before they even think it have done to this country. Gone is the sense that we have something to contribute, that our perspective is worthy of notice, that our voices and letters to Congress have an impact. I, for one, know of nothing sadder. For in this listless, thoughtless malaise we find the termites of apathy eating away at the pillars of this grand old house, this marvel of American poplar and oak, pine and maple, hewn by the sweat of patriots all. The visuals remain. They are still intact, but the trouble lies beneath the surface, for the core has been hollowed out, leaving the entire structure strained and weakened.

Fair Warning

People wrongly assume that by doing nothing, things will remain largely unchanged. Obviously, these people have never had much experience with termites. If they had, they'd realize that every day that these tiny agents of destruction are allowed to continue unabated, the whole edifice inches closer to collapsing. Denial only masks it.

The Grim Reality of our Situation is this:

We are a gridlocked nation befuddled by our method of decision making. Worse yet, we have "leaders" who have not yet attempted to tackle, let alone identify, the truly big issues that are dragging us down. It's not because these issues are hidden or are difficult to find. Indeed, they are so staggering in size and dimension that President after President has fallen into believing their own rhetoric that they are indeed powerless against them when in fact they are the ones who created them in the first place and can at any time withdraw their support.

These issues include, but are not limited to:

- *political parties that are more problematic than productive*

- *the influence of money in all aspects of our government*

- *an Electoral College that diminishes our voice in elections*

- *the giving away of most of our industrial base to China*

— *the pathetic positioning of the US as China's colony*

— *the emergence of fear–based policies in dealing with China*

— *the use of failed sanctions that only slow the advance of evil*

— *global politics that have us protect every border except ours*

— *the defeatist reasoning behind legitimizing illegal residents*

— *an economic system where the idle fare better than workers*

— *a health care system dominated by lawyers and insurers*

— *entrenched politicians who profit by making us powerless*

Wouldn't Ya Think?

Given that millions of us lost our homes and life savings, wouldn't ya think the crooks behind it would receive stiff sentences instead of bailout bonuses?

Given that our exports don't stand a chance against decades of China's unfair trade practices, wouldn't ya think we'd have import duties to level the playing field?

Given that it's been over 40 years since the OPEC oil embargo and energy crisis, wouldn't ya think we'd have a comprehensive energy plan in place by now?

Given that money has shifted power from the voters to big corporations, wouldn't ya think Congress would cleanse the temple and drive out the money changers?

Given that our oppositional two party system has now reached checkmate, game over, wouldn't ya think we'd have an intense dialogue on fine tuning democracy?

Given that this nation is as divided as were the old Civil War North and South, wouldn't ya think Congress would focus on healing our wounds as a nation?

Yet, none of it is happening. Why?

Politics as Sport

Instead of having a frank and open discussion on a topic before sitting down to take a vote, our politicians have hoodwinked us into believing we need to first toss it around and try to clobber each other in what can best be described as the great American game of political football.

Here's how it works. There are two teams complete with players, fans, cheerleaders and television commentators. The commentators whip the public into a feverish frenzy long before the contest begins, then serve as armchair quarterbacks throughout the process and remain on hand long after the contest is over.

On the field, each side focuses on scoring points against the other. This starts in the huddle where members devise plans to thwart the blocking and tackling tactics of their opponents. They can either pass it over their heads or make a run for it, barreling straight through their lines. Regardless of what they do, the opposing team has only one objective, to stop them cold. After so many downs, the other side takes possession of the ball and moves it back in the direction from whence it came.

Using the above as the framework for legislative achievement has some obvious drawbacks. First, and foremost, it divides everyone right down the middle and pits one half against the other. Second, the players run the risk of getting so caught up in the game that the issue itself is never given their full attention. And third, when both teams are evenly matched, as they are today, little progress can be achieved by either side.

Then, the whole thing bogs down into a stalemate. If the objective is sport, if the objective is drama, if the objective is increased television ratings and an ever-increasing flow of money from the fan base, then it is worth it. If, on the other hand, the objective is simply to move forward, then it is the worst possible way to succeed. Consider all of the injuries, the expenditure of time and the calories that are used to go a short distance only to have many things reversed when the other side gains control. There's got to be a better way to succeed as a democracy.

Political Parties
More of a Burden Than A Blessing

We all lose when we live in a divided country where the goal is not harmony and consensus, but rather victory over our opponents. It's like the saying, "We have met the enemy and he is us." To begin with, it means that only about half of us will ever be satisfied at any given time. It also guarantees that progress will always be slow and cumbersome if made at all. Take Amtrak as an example. Since its inception, it has been the darling of Democrats and the target of Republicans. Its funding depends on who is in office. When the Republicans are in control, funding is impeded and the whole thing deteriorates. Just when it is about to crumble, the Democrats return to power and the system is revitalized. Huge amounts of money are pumped back in, not only to restore what has fallen into disrepair, but also to sustain it through another dry spell. This is no way to run a railroad, let alone a country. Just ask defense contractors whose fortunes rise and fall on who occupies the Oval Office. It's terribly expensive to start up, shutdown and then start up again the same programs. It's like building a house and pausing just long enough for the plywood to rot a little before putting on the tar paper and shingles. Will it work? Yes. Will it pass inspection? Probably. Is it cost efficient with the best results? Definitely not.

We've been incorrectly led to believe that an adversarial relationship between two opposing parties is the only context in which a democracy can work. This simply isn't the case. Now, in a courtroom where there are only two possible outcomes, innocence or guilt, the sides are, by definition, opposed to one another. But we're not in a court of law. In fact, we're not even in the judicial branch of government. We're in the legislative branch, which, for good reason, is located on the other side of the street from the judicial. Here, consensus - not infighting - should be the goal.

We Don't Have To Play This Game

Presently we're saddled with a government where getting even the simplest of things done requires making deals. Nothing is straightforward.

Everything has strings and questionable provisions attached, but no one wants to highlight or call attention to them. Legislators just hold their breaths and vote, ignoring the repugnant, in exchange for what they see as the overall good.

While it is true that we do not have the level of graft and corruption that hogtie many other nations, we do pay a high price for the way in which our government functions within our laws. Case in point is the late Sen. Robert Byrd, a Democrat from West Virginia. He used to brag about all of the money he got for his state merely by sitting on powerful Senate committees. Nothing got past him without his blessing and his blessing often came with a price. Now multiply this "pay to play" mentality by the number of elected officials we have in local, state and federal governments and it becomes readily apparent why our nation is dripping in red ink.

Congress and Automobile Repair

The best way to illustrate this absurdity is to liken it to car ownership. For the sake of argument, let's say that the members of Congress collectively own and share the responsibility for maintaining a car.

One member notices the brakes are getting a little soft. There is plenty of brake fluid in the reservoir, but the front pads are badly worn and in urgent need of replacement. When this person mentions it and asks for the funds to fix the problem, a fellow Congressman tells him that he has his vote, but if and only if new seat covers and an exhaust system are included as they are produced in his home state. Another, for similar reasons, promises to support funding the project, but again, if and only if the battery is replaced. (There is no need for that expenditure now, but given its age, who knows, the battery may in fact fail at any time.) Still another one pledges support, but asks that the radio be updated with a new voice activated CD player and surround sound speakers.

The Representative who sounded the alarm about the urgent safety issue of driving a vehicle with failing brakes begrudgingly goes along with all of these requests, as it is the only way to get the appropriation passed. The result is an old car with repairs totaling almost as much as the car did when it was new. The other options weren't necessary, but compared to the risk of driving a car with no brakes, it was truly a good deal.

All of these distasteful little things here and distasteful little things there add up and nickel and dime us to death. Worse yet, we're not only talking about pork barrel spending. This trading of political favors back and forth is a key element of the party system and permeates the entire legislative process. We'd be shocked if we knew not how many, but rather, how few items are voted on merely on the merits of that one item. I'm not sure which is more disturbing, that this flaw has gone unabated for so long or that no one has had the wisdom, or worse yet, the courage to tackle it.

We Are Denied a Full Range of Ideas

Another problem with "politics as usual" is that we don't get the depth of wisdom our tax dollars are funding. Supposedly, some of our best thinkers are sent to Washington for the sole purpose of working through the tough problems facing our nation. Yet, instead of hearing the host of creative solutions such a gathering should produce, we only hear the same tired, limited responses day after day, week after week, no matter whose mouth is actually moving.

On the one hand, we have the conservative perspective screaming at us in unison and on the other, we have the liberal perspective screaming at us in unison. These choruses are so repetitive and predictable that if we push the mute button on our remote controls, we know, without any volume, what they are saying simply by looking at the party affiliation posted on the screen.

This shouldn't be the case. We're not getting the breadth of perspectives we need to make astute decisions as a democracy. Instead, we are spoon fed the same endless drone of carefully crafted talking points. These rob the representatives of their individual voices and deny the nation urgently needed options. Sound bites based on scripted party lines aren't going to get us where we need to go.

Where would this country be if the founding fathers coalesced around only two viewpoints as soon as they arrived in Philadelphia? The American system of government never would have gotten off the ground. Thankfully, this didn't happen. Instead, incredibly imaginative ideas spurred more incredibly imaginative ideas. Sure, there were disagreements, but they were sincere disagreements that were given sincere consideration. The issues weren't about who came up with what proposal or who got the credit. They were bigger men than that as evidenced by the fact that they just kept at it. They hung in there together despite the blistering summer heat, with no air conditioning, wearing layers of formal wool and cotton clothing topped off with hot, scratchy wigs until finally, mercifully, the whole thing came together and a nation came to birth. Now, 200 plus years later, it is sadly newsworthy that a few of our leaders were able to bring themselves to sit next to each other at, of all things, the State of the Union Address.

One of the great ironies of democracy is that sometimes small constituencies end up wielding large amounts of power. This occurs when voting blocks are split down the middle with neither side having quite enough to carry the day.

In response, both sides then seek the support of smaller, less prominent groups and promise to adopt their issues in exchange for getting additional voters to the polls. This can lead to situations where "the tail wags the dog" and can be seen even now in regions of the country where Republicans and Democrats play to Hispanics voters in order to win elections.

Some would argue this is fair play in the ruthless game of politics. I'd argue that foreign policy and determining the citizenship of millions of people is no game. Anytime the smallest group is able to exercise leverage over the majority, the nation's interests are prone to suffer. If we had issue-based governance instead of party-based governance, this would never happen. There would be no motivation for forging alliances within the government if each representative left the party system and chose to only represent the people who sent him or her to Washington to objectively examine each issue solely on its merits and nothing else. Just think how dramatically improved the process would be if this were in fact the case.

There would be no more legislating according to the wishes of some caucus meeting behind closed doors, conspiring to pass or kill a bill. Some would say this is idealistic. Bad legislation will always get through as long as mere mortals cast the votes. While this is true, take away the sport of competing political parties and we'll see just how ineffective and wildly expensive they have been. In fact, some fear that if things are not corrected, and soon, they might in short order cost us our country.

Remember, just because a lot of things "have always been this way" doesn't make them right and certainly provides no legitimacy for them to continue. There is nothing in the Constitution saying we have to use political parties. The decision is entirely up to us. The good news, the truly wonderful news, is that making a change in our operating system doesn't require a revolution, massive protests in the streets, nor even a Constitutional Amendment. It doesn't even require somehow coming up with a majority of "Independent" legislators in either the House or Senate. All that is necessary is for us as to elect individuals wherever we can, whenever we can, who see the limitations of party politics and refuse to buy into them. In time, their presence will be like the leaven in the loaf, causing the whole thing to slowly rise to new heights.

Moving Toward
Better Government

Time is of the essence. We should move with all due haste to clean house wherever possible. We need to replace as many politicians who have been involved in the game as possible and replace them with a fresh crop of individuals.

We do not need people of the same ilk, but rather people who think and act, not according to party lines, not according to power trips in Washington, not according to what will win re-election, but only according to what is good for the nation.

We need leaders with reasonable minds, good hearts and sound moral compasses that are able speak the truth in love while following their conscience and the directives of the people. That's all, and in time, other representatives will follow their examples or fade to silence until gradually, then all at once, we'll see a government of the people, by the people and for the people get traction.

There's no doubt about it. Parties are fun. They've even been a great source of amusement, particularly on the evening news, but they've cost us dearly and now threaten to reduce the greatest nation in human history to a second tier people. We won't survive this new, sobering, global configuration if we, like drunks at two out of control parties, weave back and forth from the left to the right and back again while other nations, more sober to the task, wait quietly in the wings for an opportunity to pounce.

Our most optimistic vision of our future can be found in our past. Benjamin Franklin was the consummate American. His life is still, to this day, a good example for the rest of us to follow. Listed below are but a few reasons for taking note of this friend of democracy.

1) **Ben Franklin was inventive and generous**. Many of his inventions were freely given to the public.

2) **He risked all he had to make things better.** This challenge to sacrifice is left to us today.

3) **When possible, Franklin sought the best for all,** as he felt to do less was to only partially succeed.

The Lost Art of Accommodation

Most people don't know this, but it was Benjamin Franklin who broke a stalemate that may have stopped the democratic experiment before it even got started. As history records it, the larger states understandably felt they should have the most representatives as they had the most territory and biggest populations. The smaller states, on the other hand, feared being squashed and drown out by the larger states. They had already experienced taxation without proper representation at the hands of the Crown and feared a repeat performance by the bigger states. Neither side would budge.

It was Benjamin Franklin who worked to see the validity of both sides of the same argument and came up with a solution. Instead of having only one legislative body, have two. The Senate would be comprised of an equal number of representatives from each state while the House of Representatives would have representation based on the state's population. Legislation would have to pass in both chambers before going to the President's desk for a signature. Forget about Franklin making a connection between lightning and electricity. It was his making a connection between opposing sides that was by far his greatest contribution to the American cause. He moved past the understanding of "winners" at the expense of "losers" to help form a more perfect union.

I was attending seminary in Berkeley, California when the Golden Gate Bridge celebrated its 50th anniversary. Officials closed the span and then opened it to pedestrian traffic at both ends at the same time. One end of the bridge opened with a high school marching band leading the way. At first, it all seemed well and good. Even the weather cooperated. The only problem was that no one had thought this thing through.

If they had, they would have realized that the overwhelming majority of walkers had made plans to be picked up once they reached the other side (as the span was too long for a round trip). Once these were established, there was no way to change course as there were no pay phones on the bridge and this was before most people had beepers, let alone cell phones. These folks weren't about to have friends or family members drive clear around the bay to pick them up at a pre-designated point on the other side only to find they weren't there. No, their path had been set, their destination chosen and there was no room for negotiation. They simply had to arrive.

Everything went smoothly until both groups met smack dab in the middle. Once there, what had started out as a leisurely stroll with balloons and dog leashes tied to the handlebars of baby strollers ended up becoming the pedestrian traffic jam from hell.

The poor high school marching band that had started off so gallantly ended up getting completely squashed in the ensuing gridlock. No one could budge an inch. The pressure just kept mounting and mounting as more and more piled in from both sides, pushing their way forward. It got so bad that people were actually throwing their bicycles into the pounding surf below. The total weight of the now stationary crowd flattened out the normal curvature of the bridge and more than a few wondered if the whole thing would collapse.

I relate this story because I think it is analogous to where this nation is today. We are a polarized society with a near 50/50 split when it comes to the electorate. We inevitably end up in the middle, but only to square off face to face against an equally intransigent group headed the opposite way. It is far from a joyous gathering. Rather, it is akin to getting stuck at loggerheads, dangling at a precarious height with a real fear of the whole structure falling out from under us.

What should have happened that fateful day, and should be happening every day in the halls of Congress, was to invite people to start in the middle and then move freely in either direction. Just as it is precisely the Golden Gate Bridge's ability to go with the flow instead of remaining inflexible that has made spanning the bay feasible all these years, so, too, it is in the allowance of traffic to flow in opposing directions that has made legislating the gulf that separates us an ongoing testimony to our union. The question shouldn't be "What's the best deal we can get for us?" any more than the personnel committee that was hiring my church secretary (Volume I) should have been asking "What's the least we can get away with offering?" No, in both cases, the question should have been, "What's the farthest we can go in meeting the needs and wishes of the other?"

A Few Small Changes toward Better Government

(1) Institute line item voting.

Under our current setup, bills are so large and cumbersome that no one has time to read them. This is an easy fix. Forget about getting a line item veto. Go to the root of the problem and get line item voting. That way each element is separate unto itself and there is no longer any excuse for supporting bad legislation.

(2) Don't require legislators to vote in person.

Have the bills disseminated early, via computers or on paper, so that elected officials can check off "yea" or "nay" on each provision. At the bottom they can sign off and hand them to a staffer who can then submit it on their behalf or be present on the chamber floor should the chair call for a voice vote. These simplified individual blocks of votes then become a part of their voting record that voters can scroll through when deciding whether or not to re-elect someone.

(3) Eliminate insider trading.

We don't want elected officials voting contrary to their better judgement. Doing so to pay off political favors is, in my mind, a clear conflict of interest and should be illegal. The only criteria that should be used in passing legislation is whether or not, standing on its own merits, that individual measure is for the good of the nation. Trading votes on Capitol Hill should be just as illegal as purchasing votes.

(4) Have Congress promote the nation's interests while state senators promote the state's interests.

Under the present system, each Congressional Representative's job description is in itself a conflict of interest. On the one hand, they are called upon to vote for what's best for the nation, while on the other, they are called upon to obtain what's best for their particular state. This is impossible as "no man can serve two masters."

The backroom politicking that results from this denies the legitimacy of any vote as the motivations are no longer pure. The solution is amazingly simple: discharge Congressional leaders from the task of securing the best position for their home state.

Instead, have state officials make their way to Capitol Hill to plead their cases before Congress when they have special requests like getting funding for a military base. When voting pertaining to that particular issue is taken, the Congressional representatives of that state should abstain from casting a ballot. In this way, all voting at the federal level is solely for what's in the very best interest of the entire nation, not a hodgepodge of tit for tat special favors and paybacks.

(5) No more "money-ocracy" ...our present system of government where money rules.

Take all, and I mean all, of the money out of the democratic process and return the voice to the people. This means only a set number of dollars can be used in any campaign, period. Every dime of it will come from only one source, government coffers. No more political action committees, no more corporate funding of political ads. No more leaving for long periods to raise money to get re-elected. Corporations and special interests groups can address Congress, but not with checkbook in hand through lobbyists. Rather, they can speak when they are called upon to provide information, answer questions or participate in debates for all to hear. The only time they are given voice behind closed doors is when national security demands it. This will level the playing field and keep those with deep pockets from having an unfair advantage. If these simple measures are instituted, the voice of the electorate will regain strength and our political power will no longer be sold.

(6) We should choose our elected officials instead of having them choose us.

As it is now, parties have us declare whether we are Democrats or Republicans when we register to vote. This information is then transcribed onto a detailed map that shows politicians where their bastions of support lie and helps them decide how to draw the boundaries of Congressional Districts. As might be expected, the lines are shamelessly altered to give those already in power the best chance for re-election. This "redistricting" or "gerrymandering" the territories shouldn't be legal as it comes close to openly rigging an election. The obvious and ethical solution is to dump the redistricting process altogether and replace it with a fixed grid that accommodates shifts in population.

(7) Limit the run-up to elections

There should be a cap on the length of political campaigns. Currently, people are barely sworn in before opponents are announcing a bid for their seats. How can anything get done if we never move out of campaign mode long enough to focus on business? A year is more than enough time to communicate political platforms and positions especially in this age when they can be instantly disseminated through news and internet outlets. These campaigns should only be funded by the government, period. Once we agree to this course correction, power will be taken away from multinational corporations and given back where it belongs, to the people. From that time forward, our elected officials will no longer be required to dedicate so much of their time, talent and indeed, their very souls, just to get elected.

(8) Eliminate Term Limits!

Once in a while, a truly great leader emerges. The country shouldn't be denied the gifts that person has to offer simply because of an artificial method of ensuring a rotation of power. I mean, what's the ethical difference between allowing people to compete, on the basis of abilities alone, for a second or twenty-second term? In both scenarios, their voting record during over the past election cycle should be easy to access and the citizenry should decide.

With term limits, a sitting President runs the risk of being seen as a "lame duck" even before the confetti has fully landed from the second inaugural parade.

Or, just as bad, coming from completely the opposite end of the same continuum, the President may dig in his or her heels and become a bit authoritarian now that there are no more elections to win. So once again we have created yet another dualism with the President potentially feeling either all powerful or utterly powerless. Either way, this is a needlessly self-created quagmire that has the real potential of either increasing or decreasing the authority of the office.

Furthermore, if there are term limits, adversaries here at home and abroad may be tempted to just "wait out the clock" and not respond to the President's initiatives as they know that one way or the other, someone new will soon occupy the Oval Office.

(9) Hold a special election should tragedy strike.

While it is wise to have an immediate assumption of leadership should a President die in office, I believe a special election for a permanent successor should be held.

(10) Eliminate conflicts of interest in elections.

Without question, there was a clear conflict of interest in having then Governor of Florida, Jeb

Bush, even remotely involved in the 2000 Presidential Elections. Even if there were no improprieties, the mere risk of appearing to use his office to his brother's advantage dictated that he should have been required to do what every judge does when there is even a hint of a conflict of interest, namely remove him or herself from having anything to do with the matter.

(11) Eliminate foreign money to all campaigns and all gifts to present, past or future officials.

The same China that gave, and later returned under scrutiny, money to Bill Clinton's campaign, gained control of the Panama Canal during his term in office. As President, Bill Clinton never even raised an eyebrow. Coincidence? Or money well spent?

(12) Make All Votes Equal by Taking Two Steps:

Cast Votes on Same Day/ Dump Electoral College

These two steps alone will go a long way in restoring our democracy. Under the present system, voters in Florida have far more say in electing a President than in other places. This is true for two reasons. The first reason is that the state has set up an early primary. The results from Florida's primary often determine who will stay in the race and who will drop out long before citizens in other locations get to cast an encouraging or discouraging vote.

Secondly, because of its size and number of electoral delegates, voters in Florida yield far more power than people in states like North Dakota or Delaware that have fewer votes in the Electoral College.

The fix is simple. Have two election days, one for the primary election and one for the general election. Have each vote cast on those days carry equal weight so that it doesn't matter where the vote is cast just as long as it is cast by a registered American voter.

(13) No More Filibusters

The premise of a democracy is that all voices have equal weight. Filibusters fly in the face of this as they give a single legislator the right to bring the process to a screeching halt while he or she barters for even more power. Wheeling and dealing is the problem, not the solution.

(14) No More Lobbyist Loot!

Question: Who gets paid the most attention? Answer: The people who pay the most to get it.

Our whole system of government has opened itself wide to the influence of money. As a result, we the citizens, not the multinational corporations who employ armies of lobbyists, not the foreign governments who donate to campaigns, but rather the rest of us, as in "We the People," are the ones who pay the high price for this allowance.

And when I say that we are "paying the price," I'm talking about actual dollars and cents. For the only reason, I repeat, the *only* reason, donors give to candidates and their election committees is to make their influence felt. To put it bluntly, they want the same thing any child wants, namely to get their own way.

After these "donors" are done hosting the golfing junkets and throwing the parties, "We the People" end up paying to clean up the mess. That price is always high, because there is nothing dirtier to clean up after than a government that allows the influence of money to get into its method of doing business. It taints the whole legislative process. Unfortunately, our government is just dripping with money.

How much money has found its way to our nation's Capital? It's hard to say exactly, but ask any elementary school child and they can tell you that originally Washington, D.C. was built on a swamp. (Go figure). Now, I don't know of any swamps with hills in them, do you? There aren't any. Come to think of it, there aren't any valleys in swamps, either. Legend has it that this was precisely the reason they chose to locate the seat of our government there in the first place. Our founding fathers thought that building the capital city on a swamp would mean that it would always be on the level. (So much for the best of intentions.)

Over time, however, something happened that even the founding fathers didn't anticipate, namely the infusion of money. It just started pouring in. Politicians tried to line their pockets with it, but that didn't work as they usually got caught. So they did the only thing they knew to do. They just sat on it, and in time, that pile of money grew into an entire hill of money that we've now come to know and affectionately refer to as Capitol Hill. How much money has piled up there? It's hard to reckon, but we increasingly hear it said that "Washington is just full of it."

Perhaps, this explains how they could build such a great big, heavy Capitol Building complete with that massive dome (extra storage) and yet not have it sink into the swamp. Apparently, money is holding the whole thing up. In fact, money is its only foundation. Foundation? Just listen to me, going along with their little story! I should certainly know better than to take their words at face value. But then maybe there is something behind it. After all, more and more of us are seeing the same thing. More and more of us are "holding these truths to be self-evident" that there is no real foundation on Capitol Hill other than the Almighty Dollar. Why else would commentators be forever telling us that not just the building, but the entire Hill is leaning first to the right and then to the left and back again? I don't know of anything that can cause something to sway that much unless the reports are right, that our government has raised itself to new heights, but under the fine granite, it is akin to a swamp covered cesspool filled with filthy loot.

Now, I'm no structural engineer, but given the shiftiness of money and the speed with which it moves, I think it is the absolute worst thing to use as a foundation. It's even shiftier than building a house on the proverbial sand that Jesus talked about. For money is so, what's the word? Fluid. Money is so fluid that we even talk about floating a loan, or letting the currency float until it finds its equilibrium. And we want to build on it? It all seems terribly risky given the fact that it's so slick that it can be sent around the world, via Western Union, as quick as lightning. And not only can it skedaddle, it can completely disappear. How many people do you know that scrimped and saved all their lives so that they could put just enough aside of it to build a little nest egg. Then one night, they went to bed feeling all safe and secure like a bug in a rug, only to wake up the next morning and find that poof, it was gone. And do I mean gone! Apparently the market crashed and everything was gone without so much as a trace.

No one has the billions that were lost in the crash of '29. They weren't stolen and put into someone else's account. That would have been more understandable and easier to fix. No, those billions simply vanished. They disappeared quicker than kids called upon to wash the dishes. Soon afterward, we had a housing crisis and good, hardworking people found themselves on the street. When I ponder all of this,

I'm all the more certain that I don't want my life to be built on money and I don't want the government that is there to protect and preserve my life, liberty and pursuit of happiness built on it either. We are now paying the price, the tragic price of such an error.

It's absolutely imperative that we immediately get every penny, nickel, dime and dollar out of not only every campaign, but every political activity under the sun. Until we do so, we're back to square one and the intolerable reality of taxation without representation which every reasonable patriot knows is wrong.

The preservation of democracy and the assurance of citizen participation should be job one of any President. Time on the golf links or hanging out with the elite or financially well-heeled so as to get financial contributions to win elections is certainly no excuse for ensuring the integrity of a government of the people, for the people and by the people.

Many Citizens Truly Believe
We've Gone Back to Taxation
Without Representation

How Bad has it Gotten?

Drones are clearly a major security threat and fracking is, in my opinion, nothing short of a looming environmental nightmare. Yet, to the date of the printing of this book, I'm not aware of the government promoting much public discourse on either topic. I find this to be both tragic and frightening in a supposedly democratic nation. In both cases, I think it points to the reality that money is stealing power away from the people.

Additionally, Many of Us Wonder:

Why are billions and billions given, year after year, to hostile nations that take the money and then turn around and thumb their nose at us? I find the practice repugnant. It simply has got to stop. If a country wants our help, there are things we want in return like a commitment to democratic reform. If these demands are not met, then the check will no longer be in the mail.

No More
Leaving Goodies at the Door

How much foreign aid is diverted to enrich the crooks at the top and never gets to those who are in desperate need of it? The answer is, too much. No more. We will deliver aid in such a way that it gets to its rightful destination and that it is abundantly clear that the gift is coming from us.

A Winning Strategy
for Combating Terrorism

Oct. 31, 2014, shots rang out on Parliament Hill in Ottawa, leaving Nathan Cirillo dead. He was a ceremonial sentry at Canada's National War Memorial. Following the attack and subsequent death of the shooter, the mother of Michael Zehaf-Bibeau, a self-described Muslim Jihadist, publicly denounced the incident and apologized for her son's actions.

Once again the terrorists had landed a solid punch, escaped to the supposed arms of virgins on the other side and left us with no opportunity for redress. All that was left for us to do was to begrudgingly accept his mother's apologies, comfort those impacted by the attack and brace for the loss of yet more civil liberties in a vain attempt to protect ourselves.

This scenario is certainly not new. Since September 11, 2001, this has been our ongoing response to terrorist acts.

I, For One, Do Not Accept the Major Premise of This Failed Policy

People are not hatched. They are not left to fend for themselves as best they can like lone turtles in the sand. No, they are born into families, into communities. Furthermore, individuals may be motivated by misguided self-interests to commit crimes, but they go to war for one reason and one reason alone and that reason is to better the lot of the communities into which they are born.

I submit that this gunman's acts were not, as they would have us believe, the act of a single, depraved individual. Rather, they were the composite sum total result of all the hate filled messages given him from his earliest years right up to the moment he pulled the trigger. This is based upon the simple fact that thousands of Muslims, even now, with the benefit of full disclosure of his actions, hold him up as a hero and would gladly repeat the same offense were they given the opportunity.

I cannot help but believe that though apologetic while in the media spotlight, chances are the mothers of many of these militants are privately proud of their sons and that these men are revered in their home towns in much the same way we look upon those who have lost children fighting for causes we hold dear. This undercurrent of albeit tacit approval is fully comprehended by the next generation of young boys who in turn are anxious to take up arms that they might become the next generation of heroes.

We Have Unwittingly Set Up an Unwinnable Situation

Until we accept the above premises, that terrorists are not merely individuals acting as "lone wolves" but rather are offshoots or extensions of the communities that created them, they will continue to operate with the reckless abandon of soldiers who go to war confident that retaliation for their actions will never hit home.

Indeed, they behave like children who throw a punch, knowing that all they have to do is run and hide behind their mother's apron strings. Those apron strings constitute the very same criminal justice system that was originally designed to protect innocent people from those who would intentionally and willfully harm them, not the other way around.

Here's how they use it to their advantage. After ruthlessly attacking, without the slightest provocation, unarmed and hapless civilians in a manner that exceeds any previously held estimation of savage barbarism, terrorists turn around and demand the full range of rights and privileges of a legal system that will dole out millions of taxpayer dollars to ensure they are granted a fair trial. Chances are the verdicts that are eventually reached will in all likelihood never be carried out as the same legal system views even the most painless of executions by lethal injection as cruel and unusual punishment.

Conversely, if the terrorists do happen to die during their initial assault, the whole matter is immediately dropped as we then maintain there is no one else to hold accountable. Either way, if they live or if they die, they seem to have escaped the level of wrath they unleashed on us. Thus, it is a one-sided conflict.

Moving Toward a Solution

Terrorists know full well that they are doing much more than merely committing crimes. Indeed, even the intellectually challenged can recognize the difference between a crime and an act of war. Crimes are offenses committed against individuals or groups of individuals while wars are larger in scope, hellish in nature and waged against entire societies and nations. As if we really need further proof of the difference, we need only look at how the perpetrators view their own activities. When we do this, we soon realize that even they speak in terms of jihad or a "holy war."

If a People Declares War on Us, We'd Be Foolish Not to Accept Their Assessment

Israel understands this. For decades it has been Target One, yet, even with its immediate proximity to those who seek to do it harm, it exists in relative safety. Why is that? I believe it is because they accept the scope of the conflict. They affirm that every bomb blast is an act of war committed by a warrior. In this realization, they do not call upon the police, but rather the military to deal with it. The military's response is to try to figure out who is behind the bombing, then drive a tank over and knock down their house. This suddenly changes the equation from that of a child being able to throw a punch and escape retaliation by running to the protective arms of the legal system to having the perpetrators themselves suffer real consequences. Families that once harbored terrorists now keep a close eye on their children lest their actions literally bring the house down.

They Truly Have Instigated a "War of Terror"

Since terrorists knew they didn't have sufficient wealth, soldiers or weapons to ever become an imposing military presence, they didn't even bother making the attempt. Instead they sidestepped the whole process altogether, "cut to the chase" and focused their attention on trying to create the same level of fear that the Russians felt when Napoleon's forces were advancing on St. Petersburg or Europe experienced when Hitler initiated his blitzkrieg or lightning war.

Terrorists aren't crazy. They're ingenious. Their objective is and has always been the same as every other power player, to get enough clout to become a force to be reckoned with. How they get there is ultimately irrelevant if the outcome is the same, namely to generate enough fear in others to get people to sit up, take notice and one day give in to the demands they place upon them. That is why terrorists are out to produce a level of fear so deep, so dreadful, that it can only be described as terror.

Unpredictability is Their Greatest Weapon

I firmly believe the fundamental, core component of this terror is the unpredictable nature of it all. There are no rules of engagement or codes of conduct. It has no designated battle lines, no uniformed soldiers. It can be initiated by anyone, anywhere, anytime in any number of unpredictable ways. There is no truly safe place for people to hide and take refuge. It is precisely this element of surprise, this potential for the utter banishment of serenity from our lives that makes terrorism such a scary opponent.

Yet, we need not be afraid. This challenge is definitely winnable, if we have leadership that is wise enough to figure it out and courageous enough to fight it.

Looking to the Past and Present to Chart a Future

(A Brief Aside) Congress should, and I'm serious about this, either appropriate the funds to buy out the History Channel or create one of its own. I say this because the cornerstone of any healthy democracy is an intelligent, well informed citizenry.

The knowledge base this network has acquired over the years is nothing short of phenomenal. The problem is the History Channel, for commercial reasons, shelved just about all of it and has since replaced it with endless hours upon endless hours of programing about pawn stores and the virtue of roaming the country looking for antiques and collectibles.

Had it not abandoned its original mission, perhaps we'd know some things today about Islam that might be helpful. For example, most people wrongly confuse the Spanish Inquisition with the Crusades. Though both were horrific, bloody affairs, the first was in fact an attempt to get people to subscribe to a certain theological view. The second, on the other hand, was more about access. Back then, people, including Christians, made religious pilgrimages. As Islam spread, access to the Holy Lands became threatened and the Crusades were launched to prevent this control of the region from spreading even further.

Part of the reason we blend the two is because Billy Graham used the word "crusade" to describe his efforts at spreading the Gospel. Put all of this into the same blender and factor in our knee jerk assumption that the West, particularly America, is always on the wrong side of everything and we end up with some ideas that are a bit off base. Thus the need for the kind of programming the History Channel once provided. (Now, Back to the Topic at Hand)

The Day a Flea
Took Control of a Horse

A group of thug militants appeared on the world stage 36 years ago when they stormed the US Embassy in Iran and took hostages with nothing more than a bunch of machine guns.

In terms of size and firepower against the United States, they were a bit like the flea that gained control of the horse. How did they do it? Simple. They knew that while we might be the biggest kid on the block, we were also the most ethical, the most principled and, yes, the most Sunday Schooled and it's precisely this that was their ticket to pinning us to the ground.

How did it happen? Correct me if I'm wrong, but just as some time ago we convinced ourselves we were too sophisticated for tawdry factory work, that we could make money without ever producing anything and therefore gave away all of our factories, so, too, we've not only convinced ourselves, but also put out the message to all the world that the USA is too big, too advanced, too mature and too civilized to stoop to something as barbaric, as primitive as war.

Yes. It may be true that we have the most advanced missile systems on the planet, "but with them comes the awful ethical responsibility of setting an example for the world"… and therefore will never, ever use them. Once that word was put forth, our advanced weaponry became about as useless as a high tech parking lot for advanced rocketry.

The whole dynamic reminds me of the 1940's and 50's when bodybuilders were fairly new on the scene. Back then, they were openly derided as "pretty boys" by the rough and tumble, street hardened scrappers from the likes of the lower East Side and the Bowery. They sized them up and knew these massive guys had enough strength and muscle to crush them with their bare hands, but would never do it as they were too preoccupied with their appearance to risk getting a tooth knocked out or suffering a disfigurement that would detract from posing in front of a mirror.

As it turned out, the street fighters were all about blood sport while the bodybuilders were all about image and posturing. That's just the way it was. So the littler guys with their Napoleon complexes derided and openly made fun of the much larger and more imposing body builders; and as outlandish as it seems, they consistently got away with it.

The strength of the brawlers, their secret weapon, was not their strength at all. Rather, it was the knowledge that the bigger guys would take a lot of abuse and never punch back. That's exactly what's going on with these terrorists.

Look at what each side has to bring to the fight. On the one side, we have a comparatively small contingent armed with only machine guns and crudely crafted roadside bombs. On the other side, the largest, most advanced military the world has ever known. Yet, who dominated the field? The Iranians held not only 52 diplomats, but our entire nation, captive for 444 days.

What Finally Ended the Iranian Hostage Crisis? The Answer: Good Old Fashioned Fear

As long as kind and principled Jimmy Carter was in the White House, the Iranians had nothing to fear. When Ronald Reagan came to town, the gig was up.

They knew he had no compunction about bombing the living daylights out of them if that's what it took and so out of fear of what might happen, they released the hostages the very morning he was sworn in.

Now, here we are, four decades and a number of wars later and the same terrorists that stormed the US Embassy in Iran have gone from outsiders to positions of leadership at the top. Neither they nor North Korea, another nuclear power want-to-be, have so much as a single nuclear device, yet, we're the ones who are trembling in our boots. Why?

The Reason We Are Losing the War on Terror

Quite simply, we are losing "The Terrorist War" because they're doing a better job at scaring us than we are at scaring them. Think about it. We've never threatened to wipe them from the face of the Earth, but they've never ceased talking about annihilating Israel. Is it wise to allow a nation to repeatedly make such dire threats and never throw some cautionary words back at them? I think not.

I'm just curious as to why we've never said back to them, "You'd better pray that you don't ever try something so foolish, because if you do, we will stand with Israel and you will be tossed aside and left on what Reagan once referred to as "the ash heap of history."

"Oh, that's terrible," some will say. "How could we even think of uttering saying such a thing?" And on and on it goes.

Here's my real question. Where's the leadership been? Up until now, these two bit bullies have thoroughly spooked us when they are the ones who should be worried.

Terrorists have not only threatened us, they've actually busted our lip open a few times and what has been our response? We're like the kid whose momma takes out her handkerchief, wipes away the blood, straightens out his cute little necktie, and as she combs his hair with her fingers and kisses him on the forehead tells him, "Now, don't you stoop down to their level. Carry yourself like a man so that I can be proud of you... and oh, by the way, start taking a different way to and from school."

Am I wrong? How so? We're the ones who have lost our civil liberties. Our phones are now tapped, our correspondence read, our movements tracked. We're practically strip searched every time we go to the airport. We can't even carry knapsacks or beverage coolers into crowded stadiums.... and we call ourselves Americans?

All this while the terrorists go unabated. They're actually growing in number and why wouldn't they be? We've never struck back. Oh, sure, the Bushes (in addition to plunging us into economic catastrophe every time they've been in the White House) have unilaterally thrown a few wars, but not one of them have had the slightest connection to fighting terrorism.

Any Middle East expert or child forced to repeat the fourth grade can tell you that before we entered Iraq, the country had absolutely no terrorist activity at all, period. Going into Iraq under the ridiculous guise of fighting terrorists after the 911 attacks made about as much sense as us today bombing Red Square to rid the world of Nazis. It is just about as illogical.

No, the problem is that we have responded to their war of utter unpredictability by being utterly predictable. Can you imagine being in a war where a person can lob a hand grenade and then not duck for cover, but rather immediately stand up and start walking around looking for a good defense attorney? What? They have no money to hire one? No problem. By the time it gets to court in a few years, the best of the best will be on their defense team with the American taxpayer picking up the tab.

Even if our government's side prevails in Court, the worse that can happen to them is the loss of the one person. That person can wipe out an entire city, or if Iran gets the bomb, an entire nation and the worse that will come of it is that he or she will suffer. Not at all a bad deal, is it? They can wipe out untold numbers of civilians, but we will never get more than one or perhaps a handful of convictions in a court of law.

Winning Hearts and Minds?

Why are social media companies allowing themselves to be used as the primary tool for recruiting people to join Isis? As much as I hate it when people always default to Adolf Hitler as a yardstick of ultimate evil, I am going to do just that and ask, what, if any, responsible media outlet would broadcast Hitler's propaganda today? The answer is simple. I can't think of any. Why? It is because even now it is able to incite hatred so intense as to rekindle anew unspeakable crimes against humanity.

If this is the case, how for the love of planet Earth can we even begin to justify the promulgation of such vitriolic hate mongering through social media? If the founders of these companies, the Zuckerbergs, Andersons, Dorseys, Pages and Brins of the world don't get it and continue to insist on their networks protecting terrorists' freedom of speech, then it is way past the time for governments the world over to put an end to it before further denying our personal freedoms through opening one more letter, tapping one more phone call, making one more of us practically undress at one more airport, put one more soldier in a uniform, fit one more wounded soldier with a prosthetic limb or play taps at one more funeral.

Listen to the news, read the paper. This is a war, it is they themselves who have declared it. We had better take notice and now act to try to deescalate it before it spreads past the quagmire of the Middle East to their next publicly declared target, the cities of Europe.

Who Wouldn't Go to War With Us?

Going to war with America is a pretty safe proposition. We are the last ones on the planet to acknowledge that we are under attack. As just mentioned, we deny it by trying the perpetrators as individuals in a court of law. Even worse, more often than not, we act as though nothing has happened. Just ask the Chinese who have been launching cyber-attacks on both military and civilian targets for years. Our only response, that I'm aware of, is that we've kept them on our most favored nations list. On the other side, if we accidentally miss a target, we are quick to pay big bucks to the families that have been wronged, but have some of the worst care for own veterans who are maimed for life. Need I go on?

When Will We Realize Even If We Stay on The Yellow Brick Road, It Will Only Take Us to A Fictitious Land Called Oz?

We might be arrogant and foolish enough to actually believe we can win a war by moral persuasion, but it doesn't change the fact that the very same people who strap bombs on children and send them into Crowded markets are the ones who now, as I write these words, are inching closer to obtaining legal protection for their nuclear ambitions. Having already lost our nerve, have we now also lost our minds? Why on earth would we sign onto such a deal? The argument is that by doing so, we have access to inspections, while a military response such as bombing Iran will only drive them underground. Are they kidding? Surely Neville Chamberlain could have done better.

The whole thing is eerily similar to the fallacious argument that by continuing to trade with China, not only do we have access to a formerly closed off country, but they have access to our democratic way of doing things and will easily be won over. Great! It's been almost half a century; where's this move to democratic reform? They are now curbing their citizens' access to the internet. Yet, our policy remains.

The people with whom we are dealing in Iran have not only verbalized, but demonstrated over and over again an utter disregard for human life. Quite simply, they are not to be trusted with nuclear materials of any kind for any reason, period.

So, Where Do We Go From Here?

1) We need to get off our moral high ground and realize the bottom line, namely that this is a war complete with bombs. Anytime bombs are used and nations are threatened, it isn't an individual committing a crime, it is an act of war and it shouldn't be adjudicated in a Court of Law.

2) Next, we need to realize that wars are not fought until the assailed are sick and tired of them. No, to the contrary, they are fought until the instigators get so thoroughly sick and tired of them that they will do just about anything to stop them.

3) Aggressors have no reason to stop hostilities when they are winning. Why would they stop? No, it is only after they see that it is to their ultimate disadvantage to continue that thy will call a halt to their participation.

4) We will never stop this madness until they are far more afraid of us until we are of them. The populations we are dealing with are not powerless. Look at the massive, massive,

massive turnout there was in street protests over their rage at cartoonists. They let their voices be heard. The fact that no such street protests of any kind took place in the aftermath of 911 or mass beheadings of innocent aid workers says to me they are far from innocent bystanders. None of it would happen without their support.

The cessation of their activities will only come when these same folks take to the streets and demand an end to the brutality. Whether we like it or not, that won't happen until they live under the same terror that they are dishing out to us and the rest of the world. They are the ones in the driver's seat. Once they cry enough, then and only then will the madness stop.

Lest You're Still Not Convinced, Let Me Try again... Yes, It Is that Important!

We won't negotiate with terrorists, but will negotiate with terrorist states. How does that work? I don't know. Something doesn't add up here. We take great pride in claiming the moral high ground for not negotiating with terrorists. That's all fine and good.

I, along with most Americans, most certainly don't have any problems with this and actually support it.

What I don't understand, however, is how we then go to feeling OK about negotiating with a terrorist state such as Iran. Am I missing something here? What am I not understanding? Iran, for decades, has made it abundantly clear that as a government, a county, it is committed to the "annihilation of Israel." That's their words, no one else's, and they have never been uttered by accident, as in a slip of the tongue. No, they have been stated over and over and over again in a clear, matter of fact fashion. Now, let's stop and really think about this for a moment, because it really is that important.

Annihilation. Next to eternal damnation, it is perhaps the scariest, most devastating concept human language can convey. It far exceeds even the dark loathsome pathology of the Nazis who had absolutely no compunction about exterminating Jews. As hard as it may be to imagine, this goes much, much farther in that it bespeaks the total eradication and removal of virtually everything, not just human life, so that when accomplished no people, no structures, no nature, nothing, but nothing remains.

The only, repeat only way to wipe everything so totally away is through the use of nuclear force and yet, here we are negotiating with the same state about "their right" to have a nuclear program. To even enter into such a discussion in the first place boggles the mind. That alone is bad enough, but then to be so easily hoodwinked as to accept any deal of any kind with the devil himself and then go on and suggest to potential victims that such an agreement is the only way to monitor the other side's activities so as to enable us to provide their protection is the height of repugnant folly. This isn't funny. This is serious business. Not just the citizens of Israel, not just the citizens of New York and London, Madrid and Moscow, but the citizens of any community of any density of population should be trembling in their boots, for this is far, far, far more dangerous than during the darkest hours of the Cuban Missile Crisis or any brush up during the Cold War. This a borderless war. It is about global domination. All of us, repeat, all of us the world over are at risk, for they don't need missile delivery systems, they don't even need a military. All they need is enough nuclear grade material to fill a brief case. That brief case can be left anywhere in the world by any zealot convinced there are virgins waiting for him in eternity and it's checkmate, game over. Tell me, what are you as a citizen going to do today to get our "leaders" to understand that folks like this shouldn't be handling anything even remotely connected to nuclear materials? Well? Don't just sit there. Pick up the phone, send an email, and choose wisely at the voting booth. Do all of the above, but for the love of God, for the sake of humanity, do something!

It's One Thing to Kick a Can Down the Road...

People do it all of the time. There is no real harm in it. All that happens is that the same issues are dealt with a little later on. It's quite another thing to start a snowball rolling down a hill, for it grows larger and larger and more formidable the further it travels. What started out as something innocuous can soon mushroom into something that is not only dangerous, but nearly impossible to stop.

Correct me if I'm wrong, but Iran is no empty aluminum can. Every year we don't take decisive action we allow it to become more dangerous and threatening. Like that snowball, it expands by pulling more and more into itself the further it travels. If we think the Iran of today is scary, just wait until we see the Iran of five or ten years from now.

As for Putting Putin in His Place

Administration after administration have stood silently by as this former KGB boss has slowly, but surely, worked to reverse what had been a steady movement toward true, across the board, democratic reform. We've known about his intimidation of political enemies, his gradual reduction of freedom of the press and his manipulation of the democratic process that has enabled him to remain the chief power broker despite the name changes on the door. Yet, in spite of all of this, our response has been pitifully absent. In real terms, it has been all but nonexistent.

Now, Putin, with Crimea under his belt, is threatening more invasions, and what has been our response? As of the writing of these words, it has been twofold. First, we have had our own government officials running to the microphones and quoting Putin's promise that he really and truly won't invade anywhere else. Boy that really makes me sleep better at night … and to think that Putin wants to squelch freedom of the press! Why would he want to do that when he is using it to have our leaders repeat his lies?

Our second approach is just as laughable. It is the implementation of sanctions. Are we serious? I cannot think of a situation where aggressors haven't used them to their advantage. They have rightfully come to regard them as a guaranteed time-out, not for them, but for us. Indeed, when we issue them all that registers in the ears of the offenders is our declaration that we will "give them time to work." This they accept as our promise not to strike while we are still evaluating the effectiveness of these measures.

When we use sanctions, we become like the hockey team that takes itself off the ice and sits in the penalty box while the other side carries on much as before (except perhaps a little more discreetly), firm in the assurance that nothing will be done to them militarily. What a windfall for them! They know that if they tone it down a bit and play cat and mouse, they can keep right on going without any fear of physical harm. This sense of security, of not fearing for their lives, rests not so much in their ability to protect themselves as in something even stronger, the belief that we won't break our word.

In The Final Analysis

Sanctions are to them little more than a cost of doing business, a fine, and an expensive, but foolproof way of guaranteeing their safety while they continue to operate under the protective umbrella we have offered them. Do they work? Sure they do, but only for the other side, as again, I can't think of a single instance where we have come out on top. Just look at North Korea and Iran. Thanks to sanctions, their economies are stagnant, but so what? Their leaders couldn't care less as they themselves continue to live like kings.

Both countries have made incredible strides in developing their nuclear capabilities and now we have far more reason to fear them than they have ever had to fear us. Ultimately, it all boils down to this: sanctions only slow evil's hideous advance. Perhaps that's why Webster's lengthy definition of "sanction" also includes the words "support, encouragement; approval," as in the sanctioning of a certain behavior.

What Then Will Stop
Invading Armies
in Their Tracks?

For seven decades we have borne the ginormous cost of stationing troops in Germany and the rest of Europe. Have we done it to protect us from the Nazis? I don't think so. Rather, it has been to guarantee the safety of Europe from Cold War Soviet advances. Since then, we have talked Ukraine into surrendering its nuclear arsenal by promising that we would protect them from any incursions. Well, here we are. They have been invaded by Russia and yet we have not provided them the protection we promised. How utterly pathetic is that?

To me, it is all the more grotesque given that we, at this very minute, are also pressuring Israel to trust us to defend them from Iran. Yet, year after year, we have watched Iran inch closer and closer to a nuclear bomb with sanctions only slowing, never stopping their progress. My point is this: until we back up our promises, our word is worthless.

To talk people into surrendering their defensive weapons with the promise that we will protect them and then not fulfill that promise is to sink to a new low. Such inaction is utterly amoral inasmuch as it makes us no different than those who lead the sheep to the slaughter.

The Hispanics

Even though I recognize and affirm that there are North Americans, Central Americans and Latin Americans, for the sake of brevity and readability, I have adopted the common practice of referring to citizens of the USA as "Americans." This, to my mind, is an acceptable abbreviation as only the United States includes the word "America" in its lengthy formal name.

Secondly, while angered by those who have sneaked across our borders, I welcome those who respect the rule of law and wish to join us by following due process.

Mature thinking tells us that
it is one thing to help a friend
and it is totally another
to lose one's identity
in the process.

The MAS H Generation

We live in odd times. It's as though what our teachers told us is coming true, that like ancient Rome, no foreign power can topple us. No, we can only fall from within.

Alan Alda's character did such a masterful job of training us who grew up in what I now think of as the "MASH Generation" to be cynically suspicious of all things American, that, for the first time in our history, we tend to automatically assume that we are always in the wrong and that if we aren't, then at the very least, we are doing good for all of the wrong reasons.

At the same time, we tend to naively assume the exact opposite of everyone else. We always, always, always give them the benefit of the doubt and are as blind to their shortcomings as we to the good things we routinely do. This is so deeply imbedded in our way of thinking that we now have the whole thing backwards with us assuming we are guilty until we can prove otherwise.

Are There Only
"Ugly Americans"
Or Can the Label be
Universally Applied?

The questions remain: *Why do we find it so hard to be universally fair? Why are we so blooming' accommodating when it comes to others and at the same time so ruthlessly hard on ourselves?* I don't know, but hopefully we can at least realize that only a good and compassionate people indulge in such labored self-criticism when looking in a mirror only to then turn the other cheek when looking at others.

Though we may find it distasteful to speak less than favorably of others, the fact remains that many arrive in this nation expecting total accommodation on our part to make up for a total lack of effort on their part. Nowhere is this more evident than in the refusal of some, not all, but some to learn the prevailing language and become one of us. To me, that's as distasteful as seeking to be adopted into a family and refusing to accept the family name. It is, objectively speaking, as rude as it is wrong.

A Question of Language

In order to access a computer's software, all of us commit ourselves to learning the language of computers, no questions asked, no protest made. In order to play a musical instrument such as a piano or violin, we learn the language of musical notation, no questions asked, and no protest made. When we enter a court of law, we utilize the framework and terminology of the court. There are no questions asked, no protest made. The reason we do all of these things is simple, we accept and respect the language of that particular domain. If we want to enter into it, if we want to access it, then we acquiesce to the fact that we'd better learn that language.

Adopting an official state language and allowing it to operate on one mode of expression is an acknowledgment of the State's right to enjoy freedom of expression. If people want to access governmental services, they must take the steps, as we do in the examples mentioned above, to learn the language of its expression. Remember, the State is the issuer of law and law prides itself on exactitude and minutia of meaning. Indeed, lives and generations of lives turn on the interpretation of a single word or phrase in the law. This is certainly true when it comes to the Constitution. Here we are, still struggling with the legal constructs that the Constitution presented in one language, English, well over 200 years ago. It is folly to think that our system of governance can cope with and adopt the language of every new person who arrives.

Just think of the opening for legal challenges that would be created if the government tried. Leap ahead twenty years and imagine some slick lawyer figuring out that a ballot initiative voted on years prior needs to be overturned and reversed retroactively to when it became law because it was misrepresented in one of the numerous languages that are currently used on the California ballot. Higher Courts quickly agree, apply a strict "constructionist" interpretation to the ordinance and interpret the claim by the letter of the law. Wham, millions are paid out in damages, lower court cases are subsequently reviewed and overturned and on it goes from there. It soon escalates into every lawyer's dream and our worst nightmare. Let's not go down the road. Legalisms are difficult enough as they are currently presented, with the use of just one language. Let's not make it exponentially more difficult by revisiting the tower of Babel. Let's keep it simple. When it comes to language, let's embrace the charge President Kennedy put so well, "Ask not what your country can do for you. Ask what you can do for your country."

Hispanic immigrants challenge our fundamental definition of what it means to be an American by:

1) Self identifying around a "foreign" language.

2) Coalescing around and voting for issues that only favor Hispanics and not the whole country.

When a person becomes an American, they pledge their allegiance to this nation. We all understand this. What I don't understand is how Hispanic voters can put Hispanic concerns first, over and above the concerns they have for the United States. As if to add insult to injury, both parties go right along with this crowd and play up to them in a grotesque effort to do whatever they can for their votes just so they can get re-elected. Why come to a country that prides itself, above all else, on being a great melting pot if you have no intention of joining the mix? Unless, of course, it is with the hope that everyone will eventually accept your steadfast refusal to change and/or make changes to accommodate you.

Something is terribly wrong when the new arrivals in a land flat out refuse to change. Why? Why is that so wrong? It is because at some point accommodation has to take place in order for at least some level of communication to occur. If those coming in don't learn the prevailing language and their numbers swell, then look out. It is only a matter of time before help wanted ads insist on only having bilingual applicants, or worse yet, having only those who speak Spanish apply.

Ask the natives of Miami and Los Angeles if the same thing isn't happening to them. Make no mistake about it: What we have here is a land grab without an army, a mass migration across our borders so that they can have their same lives, unchanged, that they were living in Mexico. If new arrivals won't learn English and we tolerate it, then it's safe to say that eventually, we will all have to learn Spanish. That's all there is to it.

*We Should Simply
Stop, Look And Listen!*

When people refer to themselves as "Americans" they in effect are saying, "Yes, we may be from Hungary, the Philippines or Cuba, but we all share a common political ideal, an allegiance to one country, the United States of America and therefore are *one American peopl*e. This is quite different from the second grouping of people who identify themselves as Hispanics or Latinos and say, "Yes, we may be from El Salvador, from Mexico, from Guatemala, but we all speak a common language, Spanish, and therefore are *one Latino people."*

When I look at the old film clips of people sailing into New York Harbor a century ago, they were all waving little American flags before they even set foot on American soil. From that point on, they always referred to their former homeland as "the old country" and gladly threw themselves into the blending that transformed all them into a new breed of human beings. In short, they became Americans.

Canada has always been about being this great patchwork of diversity and has supported bilingual education and other forms of the multi-cultural experience. Well, guess what? What began as an affirmation of diversity soon became an opening for separatists to get a foothold and sure enough, our worst nightmare has already occurred there. The Anglophones, those who speak English, are no longer comfortable in Montreal and are leaving the province as they feel like strangers in their own country. French is now the dominant language.

The Crux of the Problem

Many Hispanics feel entitled to the southern U.S. They do so pointing out that much of California and Texas were originally part of Mexico. While yes, this is true, it is also true that it was barren, undeveloped land before we came in and transformed it into what it has become today. The fact that many Mexicans in Mexico feel this way is scary enough. To then realize that the same view is held by Hispanics within our borders is even more frightening, given the fact that they now are the largest demographic group in California. It only goes to follow that, as the majority, they will one day want to force the state and possibly the nation to become bilingual.

Hispanics have already set up their little enclaves of Mexico right here in the US. This has created a situation where the people in Altoona, Pennsylvania or Miami, FL. or Los Angeles, CA. had better be prepared to speak Spanish when they go to the store or they may well return home empty handed.

I experienced this firsthand when I lived in Manhattan. There was a little "mom and pops store" directly across the street from my apartment building. I tried to get some essentials there once and found that none of the items had prices on them. When I asked how much for this or that, it became apparent that they didn't speak English so I couldn't buy anything. As I was leaving, I couldn't help but notice their total indifference at losing a sale.

It was clear that they felt it was purely my loss, not theirs. Over the years, they had developed a whole clientele of Spanish speaking people who had also become part of their insular little community and accordingly couldn't care less if I didn't shop there.

Is It Ethical to Deny Benefits?

It is once we recognize that nations are groupings of people, like families, or, if you like, condominium associations where individuals contribute to the whole with the assumption and reasonable expectation that the proceeds and subsequent benefits will not be dispensed to the world at large, or even to those who drop in, but rather will be reserved for those who by name and title are legally a part of that said union. Go ahead, try to find someone who can't understand that. A lot of people may not like it, but I'd venture to say that most, even if only privately, would accept this as an accurate and fair rendering of the issue at hand.

The Problem Is That We Have Turned The Whole Thing Completely Upside Down!

As impossibly backwards as it seems, most of us could accept this if the situation were reversed and we were the ones being denied benefits in a foreign land. Yet, when it comes to us standing up for ourselves and saying no to those who seek to draw from tax collected funds to which they have never contributed, we have a difficult time saying no. Why do we do this? How can we justify it? Remember: for something to be truly ethical, it must apply to a wide array of situations. In light of this, I remind us of the admonition to love our neighbors as ourselves.

Catch and Release
Is For Fishing
Not the Border Patrol

Why in the world would people stop crossing into the United States if the only penalty is a free flight home? The answer is being played out every day. They wouldn't! They just keep on coming back over and over again. How stupid can we be? As I see it, we can: (a) spend an infinite amount of money building a fence, that can be breached across hundreds and hundreds of miles, (b) continue to hand out free plane tickets home to the tune of millions of dollars a year, or (c) give ample warning, have it broadcast loud and clear and then have the Federal Government impose stiff five year sentences for those who cross into the country illegally. A small number may incur the sentence, but I doubt very many. It is a lot more humane and ethical than not having a strong deterrent and as a consequence continue to sit by and watch people die from trying to cross such an unforgiving terrain.

The Canadian
Guest Worker Program

It works because it is based on common sense. If Mexicans want to bypass the mess we have created for seasonal workers here in the US, they can contact Canadian authorities stationed in Mexico who, in turn, are able to match them with specific employers in Canada. Upon agreeing to the terms of their employment, these guest workers are given a plane ticket with the firm expectation that upon arrival they are to report directly to their employer, work at the agreed upon task and then, upon completion of the task, use the return portion of their ticket for their flight home. A failure by the worker or the employer to live up to their end of the bargain results in disqualification.

This is currently is in place in Canada as outlined in a lengthy segment broadcast on National Public Radio. When interviewed, both the workers and their employers stated that they loved it. When the program then went on to ask American officials their reaction to it, they were the ones who uttered disapproval. Why? Because they said it denied workers the flexibility to seek out a better situation if it didn't work out well with their employer. My response to this is that (1) even though it was not spelled out in the segment, I'm sure they have a grievance/mediation process in place precisely for such situations and (2) even if they don't, we must remember that this is only for a season.

I'm also sure employers are well aware that word circles quickly among workers as to who is and isn't a good employer and they don't want to be in the latter category as the next time around they don't want to go without a sufficient number of workers or be supplied with only the ones no one else will hire.

A Simple Plan
Our Policy Makers
Reject

Why? What is their reason? It denies workers their rights to shop around for something better once they arrive in the host country. Are they serious! If we open the door to our homes to folks we have never met before, we don't let them meander through the house and do as they please. No, if they have come to fix the water heater or paint the hallway or even use the bathroom, we either lead them to it or give them directions as to its location. But we don't stop there, we keep tabs on where they are until they leave. It's only logical!

There we have it. Here we are wondering why so may now enter our country and then blend into the scenery in L.A. or Miami, never to be seen again until they either seek permanent residency status or a green card, need medical care or get arrested. This is the reason. We throw open the doors and don't have in place a way of verifying their whereabouts once they get here. The ugly truth of the matter is that if it were not for political parties, we wouldn't be discussing immigrants outnumbering our citizens.

Instead, we'd be voting to cut off benefits and deny them work. Yet, the parties are resistant as it seems they value their own survival more than our survival as a nation.

Who Said Anything about Using Gestapo Like Round-ups Tactics?

Don't fall for the lies and terrible accusations of those wanting to ignore the integrity of our borders. They are quick to assert that the only way to get all of these people back to their home country is to resort to Gestapo like tactics complete with the mass rounding up of civilians, internment camps and other brutal measures similar to those used during World War II and earlier in history during the Veil of Tears. Talk about cheap shots! I find such ludicrous allegations to be as hate filled as they are utterly ridiculous. If we were such cruel and callous people, why would anyone even consider moving here in the first place? It's illogical.

Once we stop benefits to illegal recipients and actively work to improve living and working conditions in Mexico, they will start to migrate southward to their home country. This is not unfair. It is far more charitable and humane than many, if not most, countries would do under these circumstances. Again, if we were in another nation's borders illegally, there isn't a person among us who would find fault with us not getting benefits that were only intended for the pool of people who paid into their system. So, why is this any different when we are the country in question?

America, don't you dare cave in on this one! It is your country, dog gone it! Don't fall for the cheap guilt trips laid upon you by usurpers who have no legitimate right to be here. Their claim is as ridiculous as Indians showing up in Manhattan with a receipt and the trinkets used in the original transaction hoping we will give them the island. If this makes sense, why not just give the whole thing back to the Vikings?

People who have taken it upon themselves to either sneak in or stayed past their scheduled date of departure are the ones who should feel guilty, not us. They have no more right to our country than a passerby has the right to the keys to our homes or the money in our pensions.

Do whatever it takes to "preserve, protect and defend" not only the Constitution, but our country, "from all threats, both foreign and domestic." Rise up and vote out of office those candidates who would partial out this land incrementally neighborhood by neighborhood, city by city and state by state to those who wish to come here and set up offsite outposts of their native homelands. This country is not for sale and most certainly is not to be given away. The door is open, but it is only open to people who are willing to surrender any and all ties to former nations in order to pick up their new, all-consuming identity as Americans.

US Protects Every Border Except Ours?

There must have been a typo somewhere along the line for the US Military has somehow become the UN's Military. Now, a border incursion anywhere in the world sets off an immediate call for our deployment. This is not done lightly, however, as we won't act without first forming a "coalition of the willing" … as in a long list of nations more than willing to let us do all of the heavy lifting. Yes indeed, thanks to our tax dollars, people the world over go to bed feeling secure … unless, of course, they live in Arizona, Texas, California or Florida. For our troops are stationed to provide maximum protection for any international border except, of course, our very own. How do we justify this?

Isn't It Odd?

We don't fault Australia for denying entrance to anyone and everyone who can't pay huge amounts of money to move there, but we beat ourselves up for seeking to stem the flow of penniless immigrants who now number in the millions in California. Why such a cruel, self-hating double standard?

Three Questions for Consideration

1) What would Canada look like without the Province of Quebec? Why do I ask? It's because it almost happened not too many years ago. It's true. They had a very close election and it may come up for a vote again.

2) What would Great Britain look like without Ireland? Why do I ask? It's because it almost happened within the past year. It, too, was a real squeaker of an election and could have gone either way with Ireland becoming independent.

3) What would the United States look like without California? Why do I ask? I don't know, other than to remind us that maps are redrawn all of the time. Just as Canada would have been severely be crippled if Quebec had just a few more votes in favor of succession and Great Britain would be forever diminished if the vote in Ireland had gone the other way, so, too, I shudder to think what this country would look like without its West Coast.

Any nation that allows foreigners to outnumber its own citizens is doing nothing short of creating the perfect environment for a revolt in either the voting booth or on the field of battle.

Do we really have to wait until there is an actual ballot initiative for secession similar to those in Canada and Great Britain before we realize how potentially dangerous it might be to just hand over a majority vote to a people who have never expressed an affinity for the country as a whole?

What About Our Government's Promises to its Own Citizens?

It's only ethical that the Federal Government honors its original promise to its own people before making any more. Before we look at this government's request to grant a blanket across the board amnesty to those living here illegally, let's look at the first time it asked for the same thing in 1986. I remember it clearly, but for those who don't, let's haul out the newspaper and television news accounts of that period. Do this and we'll see that this country has been more than generous. It went to ridiculous lengths to make sure every illegal alien had the opportunity to become full fledged American citizens with one caveat, that this offer would never be repeated again. That was the promise, the sales pitch, and on the basis of this promise, votes were cast.

Now, here we are 28 years later and we're back to square one. The only difference is that back then there were 3 million illegal residents in question. Today the number has swelled to four times that amount. Yet, the President and Congress assure us this will solve the problem of illegal immigration. Why on Earth would they think that? Better still, why on Earth would we believe them now?

It raises for me the question, "What right does the government have to violate its promise to its people?" It also leads me to suggest that if the original agreement was unfair or faulty, then fine, let's go back and revoke it. We'll just pretend that it never happened and retroactively nullify every citizenship paper that was issued under that agreement. Not fair? Why not? They can't have it both ways.

Two Parables

Once upon a time...

there lived two neighboring families. One had created a nice life for themselves. Everything had its place and was in order. As a result, their home became the envy of the neighborhood.

Immediately next door, life was not so good. It seemed that they lived in a constant state of disarray. Doors were left open, the lawn was never kept up and mowed, the children lacked discipline and the drama encircling their lives never seemed to wane. The contrast between the two neighbors could not have been more obvious.

It was only a matter of time before the children from the house of disarray started spending more and more time next door. They enjoyed all the niceties life at home failed to afford them and so it only made sense that they gravitated in their neighbor's direction. After all, it was a quick fix. All they had to do was travel the short distance and suddenly their lives dramatically improved to the extent that they never wanted to go home.

For a while this arrangement was acceptable, but in time two things were noticed. First, it didn't improve anything in the house of disarray, the source of their discontentment. Secondly, it was only a matter of time before their way of living impacted their neighbor's. Soon they were dealing with behaviors their guests brought with them and now instead of one house in disarray, there were two. The solution was not for the one family to walk away from their situation, but rather to address it and correct it there.

Again, once upon another time...

there lived a gentle giant. Its strength was unequalled and nothing could escape the length of its grasp. All of its neighbors came to rely on its strength and gentle benevolence as it had a special place in its heart for the weak, the defenseless and those in need of assistance.

In time, however, lesser forces around it came to realize that even a giant is itself vulnerable for giants tend to have giant hearts. Get to that heart, cause it to question its motivations and become inwardly conflicted and soon it will lose its strength of confidence.

That giant is not at all unlike the United States. It, too, needs a word of encouragement now and then, for no nation has had a bigger heart and gentle giants like this one are few and far between.

Will California Become Another Crimea?

Consider Crimea. Here we have a situation where people within Ukraine's borders had a deeper love for the neighboring country than they did for the land where they lived. In time, they voted to be annexed into that neighboring country. What's to keep the same thing from happening in this situation with Hispanics within our borders? Or again, as the new majority, why wouldn't they insist on the adoption of their native tongue, Spanish, in all aspects of life including all speeches in the halls of Congress and the printing of bilingual currency?

The question then transitions to that of why? Why would we freely give away our homeland to a foreign people who, unless they are abnormally different from every other grouping of people, would naturally move to secure this land as theirs and alter its institutions to reflect them, thereby making us feel like foreigners in our own land? Why? Why? Why?

Logic Itself Calls Us To Consider The Following:

1) Given that these immigrants have persisted in keeping Spanish as their primary language when they had no power, what leads us to believe they will start speaking English once we give Hispanics a majority vote in California by making them US citizens?

2) Again, haven't we been watching the news? Nation after nation is being divided along linguistic lines. Do we really want to run the risk of becoming yet one more country to reaffirm a great truth uttered by none other than Jesus Christ who warned that "a house divided cannot stand?"

3) If we couldn't keep the door closed and secure California's border when Americans were in the majority, what on earth makes us think the door won't be opened even wider with a Mexican majority that will naturally want to have their families join them?

4) Minors should assume the same legal status as their parents. If the parent is an illegal resident,

then the child is an illegal resident. This only makes sense.

Fix the problems where they are, in Mexico. Flee from them and they will surely follow.

We Do Need to Be the Very Best of Neighbors.

Mexico is a mess and our addiction to drugs is not solely, but largely, responsible. The solution is not for Mexicans to flee north as that will only worsen things there and go on to create a myriad of problems here.

Let's stop encouraging far flung people to walk away the challenges they face. Instead, let's assist them in finding real solutions. We need to redirect aid from hostile nations and send those funds to help our neighbors to the south. For we really do need to pitch in and do our part, but we need to do it in such a way that really and truly helps Mexico while at the same time honoring the vision of our nation, namely that we remain a melting pot, not a collection of separate people!

We Should Affirm Our National Motto: E Pluribus Unum (Out Of Many One)

We should ponder, meditate on, take stock of and live up to our National Motto: E pluribus Unum"…..Out of Many One. It is a powerful statement, a vision our founding fathers (and mothers) had for this country and a sobering acknowledgement of the simple fact that in order to pick up and fully embrace something new, a relinquishing, putting down and walking away from things previously cherished must first take place. It is akin to the vows in a wedding ceremony where all else takes a back seat to the supremacy of a love between two people.

This theme is not only verbalized, but literally acted out in the actual staging of the ceremony which, like a play, opens with the bride being escorted in by her father. His presence represents her family and her life up to that point. It affirms the past and yet there is a poignant moment when he stops and withdraws once the bride reaches the front of the sanctuary and joins her future husband. Yet, she is not the only one called upon to leave the past behind and make sacrifices as during the ceremony the groom is also admonished to leave his father and mother and cleave only to his wife.

Once the couple is positioned together, standing side by side, this theme of separating, of pulling away from all other concerns is advanced again, this time by the congregation who is asked if they know of any previously held allegiances or any "just cause" why these two cannot be joined together. This settled, the couple is then bid to move even further ahead in their shared path of exclusion, this time away from even their closest friends, their maids of honor and groomsmen until they finally arrive at the altar. It is there that they alone, in a very intimate, but public moment, take solemn vows and declare to the world that through thick and thin, good times and bad, they are in it until death do they part.

Then and only then are they spun around and reintroduced to their friends and family as if for the very first time. They are now a new reality, a new family unit with a new name and identity, ready to face the blessings and challenges that lie before them.

Emboldened with a joy rooted in confidence, they do not walk; they do not mosey or saunter, nor prance or dance. To the contrary, they boldly march, arm in arm to the triumphant strains of "the wedding march" right through the middle of the crowd stopping for no one or no thing and keep right on going out the doors of the church and into the glistening reality of the new life they have established together.

Against this backdrop, I look at the illegal immigrants who have arrived here in our midst unannounced and uninvited. They say they seek the blessings of a new relationship, but have been unyielding in their utter determination to surrender nothing and remain the same as before they broke our laws by crossing our borders. They want to keep their "proud Hispanic heritage," their way of life, their language, even their right to continue voting in Mexican (as well as) American elections. Each one of these actions on their part only reaffirms the obvious fact that they don't want to have anything to do with becoming part of our grand union. Having heard and witnessed their endlessly reaffirmed deep down decision to remain unchanged, we need only feel entirely comfortable in saying to them with equal clarity of voice, "Adios and Good bye."

My Take on the Presidency

A great President is one who is able to see things far enough ahead to steer this massive ship of state away from the rocks and into deep majestic waters where it can stretch its legs. It's about seeing the much bigger picture and sharing the vision, then taking decisive steps to achieve it while at the same time exuding the joy and confidence that bespeaks the best of what this nation has to offer.

We live in troubling times, when the great visionaries of the age have either gone on before us or all but lost their voices. Yet, I am confident that the same hope that has seen us through tougher times will see us through yet again. It is alive and well in the American classroom where children are still taught that justice is not expendable and virtue has a price. It is the promise of the living uttered at memorials to fallen heroes that their sacrifice will not only be remembered, but held high as an inspiration so that when our time comes, we will not falter.

Since Lincoln, no incoming President has had the challenge of healing the wounds of such a deeply divided land. Indeed, it is this division, this inner turmoil and angst that threatens to render us powerless against the challenges we would otherwise find so infinitely surmountable.

As a good and noble people, we are quick to evaluate and judge ourselves by standards we would immediately feel harsh in applying to others. This has caused us to sink into the phantom pain of misplaced guilt that lesser nations have placed upon us in an attempt to dodge their own much needed introspection.

I take up the challenge their brooding thoughts illicit. Let me, as an ever proud American, tell you about this country and its people. It is, to the very best of my knowledge, the only nation in recorded history that routinely rebuilds the countries that have savagely waged war against it. Am I wrong? What other nation, either today or in history, has ever done so. I very much doubt one can be named.

Then, there is the shame that should be upon us for the awful names we have called our enemies in the heat of battle. We have called the Japanese "Japs", the Germans "Gerry's" and communists "commies." How terrible, abbreviating their names like that. Why, it is every bit as bad as calling the folks in Oklahoma "Okies!" Shame on us.

Name a nation that is as reluctant as this republic to go into battle, and when it does so is almost always there solely to lend support to a nation under siege. Take Viet Nam, the birthplace of much of this inner self-loathing, as an example. History bears witness to the simple fact that we had nothing whatsoever to gain in that conflict. We reluctantly went in for purely humanitarian reasons as there weren't any economic or territorial incentives to be gained. We went in for one reason and one reason only, namely to support the South Vietnamese who were under attack from communist forces.

The same defensive role was taken by us in the previous decade on the Korean Peninsula, when once again, communist forces in the north attacked the democratic forces in the south. In both conflicts, the United States was simply trying to stop the real, not merely perceived, but real spread of global communism. Had the US elected not to do so, it would not itself have suffered as it was more than able to defend itself from any real or perceived threat in that era.

Indeed, the US could have returned to the comfortable quiet life of the Eisenhower years, but didn't. Instead, it stood up for vulnerable South

Vietnam against the onslaught of the North even though it did long term damage to our own sense of who we are and what we are about.

We forget that in August of 1961, the communists put up the Berlin Wall. Only fourteen short months later, in October of 1962, we had the Cuban Missile Crisis. These events took place at the very same time that Soviet Premier Nikita Khrushchev was verbally haranguing the United Nations with his support of taking these aggressive measures global.

To recap, there were aggressive acts on the part of communists in the Western Hemisphere (Cuba), in Europe (Berlin) and in Southeast Asia (Vietnam). The only force positioned to stop them was the United States. Given that the communists did prevail in Cuba and Berlin, I certainly understand our refusal to stand idly by and watch them prevail in Vietnam. I, for one, am grateful to those who fought for the defense of individual freedom in that land. We may have lost that battle, but I'm wise enough to know that the larger war, the war for the right to self-determination, is far from over. There's no doubt in my mind that without the extreme sacrifice of those who fought, suffered and died, other incursions would have taken place.

Enough said. I am not in denial about our shortcomings. This book speaks volumes about our flirtation with greed and the recent loss of our moral compass. At the same time, however, I will probably be the very last person to ever give up on us. And even if, God forbid, we do not now find permission within to pick ourselves up off the mat and fight for our nation, my hope and prayer is that we will at least rise up in defense of a troubled world that would sorely miss the most generous, self-effacing ally it has ever had. With this in mind, I, with all that is within, pray that God will continue to direct, forgive, ennoble and bless this mighty land.

Two Notions Politicians Routinely Peddle:

1) *They're nobler than the rest because, unlike their counterparts, they're the ones who are "working within the system for change."*

2) *Accordingly, from time to time, they have no choice but to make compromises. They do so reluctantly, however, as part and parcel of the on-going heavy price they routinely suffer to advance the nobler causes they were sent to Washington to address.*

This pretty much covers it, doesn't it?

If folks like what they do and how they vote, then that's wonderful. If voters don't approve, that's still OK because politicians can always claim they had to do it to stay in place for future battles.

It's a bit like having a police force, or better yet, a military that proudly boasts it will do whatever it takes to protect the country just as long as its soldiers are never in harm's way. And why is that? We are told it is because the generals have to ensure the safety of their soldiers in order to keep them for our protection in the future...just as long as, like today's encounters with the enemy...they remain completely safe and free from danger.

This line of thinking is eerily similar to today's professional, career politicians. They suffer from a collective delusion of grandeur, the deep seated belief in their own political indispensability which in turn has led to the erroneous notion that we cannot possibly make it without them. Once this thought is firmly entrenched in their minds and hearts, we see that everything is negotiable when it comes to keeping themselves and their political party in power.

Final Thoughts on Forming a More Perfect Union

I want more than anything for us to continue on as a democracy, but in order to do so, we have to dump this dysfunctional way of doing things. Quite simply, if the only way we can get beyond our inner desire to take up sides against each other is to have our government fund athletic teams, then let's do it. That is more than fine with me, but for goodness' sake, let's get this mentality of competing out of our heads when it comes to drafting legislation. For in the final analysis, it shouldn't boil down to winners versus losers. It should come down to knowing beyond any reasonable doubt that we as a people have come as close as possible to making clean, well thought out choices.

Again, the crux of the problem is the process. I am convinced that once we stand far enough back from it to see just how self-defeating it has become, we'll hopefully see through this ridiculous practice of dividing ourselves up, going to opposite ends of the field and commencing to run headlong into each other at full tilt only to later question why, all stymied and bloody, we don't get farther.

No wonder other nations are pulling ahead. It's as though we have somehow convinced ourselves that we must always dwell in a scaled back version of the Civil War, except of course, and on those rare dates like December 8, 1941 or September 12, 2001, the days immediately after we were savagely attacked. At least on those days we were one people, united together, waving American flags and singing God Bless America instead of squaring off in opposing camps.

The haunting image I have in my mind's eye of the United States' situation today is that we are tragically like a football stadium filled with spectators who are so caught up in the competition on the field that they fail to pay adequate attention to the fact that just outside the arena, opponents, in this case the Chinese, have surrounded the entire complex and are positioning themselves to move in for the kill.

Clearly, our political process has become too inwardly focused, too energy absorbing and too distracting to meet the needs of a 21st century nation that must immediately pull out of its nose dive if it is to have any hope of surviving.

Why don't we keep the free speech, keep the frank dialoging, keep the decision making of the people, for the people and by the people and then go the next step and dump the whole notion of putting ourselves on teams. For as long as we have teams, be they Republicans and Democrats, or what-have-you versus what-have- you, we will by definition be a nation divided. Why not only have only one team and as one team only have one adversary, evil? Hey, it worked for the writers of Superman, you know, "truth, justice and the American way." It all makes sense to me.

If only we could do this, I think we'd make old Benjamin Franklin, George Washington, Thomas Jefferson and the whole gang back in 1776 all the more proud. For then we will have reclaimed the essence of what they were about. It's not the influence of money or power or prestige, nor is it about getting one's way. To the contrary, it is about emptying ourselves of our own interests that people in power might hear and lend voice to the average citizen. After all, the quest of the American Revolution was to form a government so reflective of the people it served that its members were not given titles consistent with royalty, but rather the more humble title of a House of Representatives.

OUT

OF

KILTER

The War on Poverty

Won't Be Over Until

People Are Autonomous,

Self Directed

And Most Importantly

Self Sufficient.

Continuing Forward!

Thanks to the bravery and life work of the Reverend Dr. Martin Luther King Junior, blacks are finally in the house. That's great! Wonderful! Yet, the work is far from over.

It won't so much as begin to near completion until we stop enabling, allow for the assumption of responsibility and begin to transition people from the kiddie table into the real, adult world of self-reliance.

They obviously can do it. We just have to step aside a bit and let them cut their own meat and make their own decisions while we actively cheer them on.

It'll require a collective effort, but that's O.K. We're all in this together. After all, we truly are part of "the Human Family."

Dangerously Out Of Kilter

The first, very first, thing God did was work an honest week. It's true! Dedication to the task became pride of accomplishment, which was then followed by Sabbath rest. Wanting to share the joy, God immediately sent man to tend a garden that we, too, might reap the same benefits. Most of us get it. Most of us understand that the best feeling in the world is receiving good pay for a job done well.

Regrettably, however, there are those who don't. They skip over the part about working and want to go directly to rest. They want to enjoy the fruits of labor, just long as it's not their labor. So, they pile on and take a free ride on those who pull their weight through the sweat of their brow. Accordingly, honest wage earners are hit from all sides, both coming and going. On their shoulders, they carry the weight of employers and financiers whose bloated pay packages are often determined by their ability to deny fair compensation to those who have rightfully earned a decent living.

Then, coming from the exact opposite direction, but armed with the same combination of greed mixed with slothfulness, are those not at the top, but rather the absolute bottom, who contribute as little as possible, save their own bad life decisions, and then play on our sympathies, hoping and trusting we will have pity and perpetually support them. These individuals, directed by impulses and not long range planning, drop out of school, sabotage their lives, and have us care for them.

So, there we have it, those who rise early and faithfully go to work every day continue to lose ground because they are saddled with the weight of those perched on their shoulders and the weight of those clinging to their ankles as they trudge forward, just trying to make ends meet. Truly, folks caught in the middle are getting the rawest of deals.

We Need To Pause, Stand Back and Look at the Kind of Life We Have Created

Something is not right when people refrain from earning above a certain amount of money lest they lose their benefits. Yet, that is exactly what is happening today. Literally millions of Americans have counted the cost and determined it is in their best interest to remain just idle enough and poor enough for the rest of us to carry them in perpetuity.

Something is not right when companies refrain from hiring above a certain number of people lest they enter a new bracket that requires workers' comp and health insurance for their employees. Yet, there isn't a fledgling enterprise in this country that hasn't seriously considered holding itself back lest the cost of doing business becomes prohibitive.

Something is not right when people have to work at multiple jobs because their employers won't schedule them for more than 32 hours a week as a way of avoiding paying health coverage. Yet, it is happening more and more often in this land of opportunity.

Something is not right when American companies have to pay a major portion of their employees' insurance while competing against global rivals that don't, yet that is the reality in this "new world order" that Administration after Administration have pushed on us.

Something is not right when people do all of the right things, make all of the right choices, endure all of the right sacrifices, and work hard art-in and year-out only to end up homeless one day due to the loss of their jobs, and the subsequent loss of their medical benefits ... while others who have never worked a day in their lives or taken any responsibility for their actions, are guaranteed perpetual food, shelter, and limitless health care for themselves and their dependents. Yet, we see it all of the time.

I believe it is in everyone's best interest to have a country where we all work and play, live and die on the same level playing field, where the decisions we make have real consequences and create real opportunities.

Ultimately It All Boils Down to a Fork in the Road

Option I:
We can continue to develop larger and larger societal systems where all of our time, effort, and resources go into erecting and maintaining a massive network that supplies all of our needs or…

Option II:
We all try to simplify things at every level and make life as fair as possible so that each is person is afforded the opportunity to make the best out of his or her own personal life. The first approach of

devising ever larger societal programs to fix our personal needs disempowers the individual as their power is funneled up to the top of the pyramid from which all decisions are made. The bigger the structure, the less personal decision making and freedom are tolerated.

I am of the opinion that the second option-- personal freedom—is better as it enhances drive and creativity instead of stifling them. It assumes the best of people instead of the worst and doesn't waste a majority of its efforts on crowd control and the policing of its own people.

To Regulate–Or Not To Regulate?

The Answer is Simple:

- *Regulate the things that are so big that people are powerless against them.*

- *Deregulate the things where doing so makes people more independent and self-reliant.*

For example:

We do need strictly enforced regulation of the business community, as without it, consumers are at their mercy. At the same time, we're best served by the deregulation of price and fare structures as this promotes competition and keeps the lid on price hikes.

Republicans: Listen Up!

No one can make sure that banks and Wall Street play by the rules; no one, save regulatory bodies that were created to do just that. When they fall asleep on the job, greed runs amuck and shady practices cause millions of people to lose their life savings.

We saw it happen in the Depression, the Savings and Loan debacle of the 1980s, the stock market crash that occurred later in the same decade and the mega real estate and stock market meltdown of 2006-8. Perhaps we will now take seriously the need to police those who handle our money.

Democrats: Listen Up!

Conversely, while we obviously do need large scale monitoring of large scale enterprises--lest the little guy gets trampled--the exact opposite is true when we as a society are tempted to get overly involved in the daily needs of people's personal lives.

The more society as a whole tries to step up and fix people, the more we see a large percentage of them draw back and allow us to do just that. In fact, it is becoming increasingly evident that when we "give a man a fish," we often not only end up feeding him for a day but an entire lifetime.

The reason for this is simple:

People know that the more we provide for them, the less they have to do to care for themselves. As a result, their economic situation often doesn't improve, but rather gets bogged down in ever deepening dependency. They come to wrongly misinterpret these unexpected blessings as an opening for working less.

Forgive the analogy, but this dynamic closely resembles the experience of park rangers at Yellowstone National Park. Over the years, bears were beginning to lose their natural ability to hunt because they were hanging around the campgrounds, eating freebies from the dumpsters. The more this went on, the more park rangers had to make drastic changes in their waste management practices--not for their sake or the tourists' sake, but for the sake of the bears.

The same principle applies here. We should have people take responsibility for their own lives and pay for the things they can personally afford. This will deter people from making irresponsible decisions and becoming dependent on the state for assistance.

What about Our Responsibility to the Poor?

I believe I do have some life experience here. I was raised in a middle class family in suburban Maryland. My father was a pastor and my mother was an elementary school music teacher. When I was 18, I moved to Koinonia Farm, a Christian Community seven miles outside of Americus, Georgia. (The name Koinonia comes from the Greek word for fellowship.)

While there, I got involved in a literacy program for youngsters and within a few months of my arrival, I moved into the poorest section of town and became a neighborhood big brother to the very kids I had been tutoring. I wanted to live on or below the economic level they did, so I supported myself by working part time at Hardee's.

I rented a concrete block shack for $20 a month that I affectionately called the Shady Rest. In looking back, I should have come up with a better name as there was little rest with the occasional freight trains running less than twenty feet from my front door. My furnishings consisted of one chair, a bureau, and a box spring on a bare concrete floor. I had no radio or television, just a single naked light bulb hanging from the ceiling, a sink that only ran cold water, and a flush toilet in the equivalent of an outhouse. I existed on one meal a day at the local college where, a couple of times a week, I sneaked the world's fastest showers. I don't know of a time when I've ever been happier.

Twice a week, "my kids" came over for Bible stories, refreshments and a hike to the library where the most wonderful staff in the world reached out and simply loved them. They read children's stories to them, put on puppet shows, and went out of their way to make sure every child got a library card whether the books were returned or not. In time, the Shady Rest became a bookmobile stop.

When Linda and Millard Fuller returned from a couple of years of building houses in Zaire, on behalf of the fellowship at Koinonia Farm, Millard opened a law practice and started a new global housing ministry. In exchange for painting his house, he offered to let me stay rent free in a back room of the office, thus making me (without ever working there) the very first resident of Habitat for Humanity.

Since then, my life has been largely about serving others. I have spent years working to provide adequate nutrition to impoverished seniors, words of hope to the incarcerated, and a way out for heroin addicts in the South Bronx, which at that time was described by ABC News as "the worst neighborhood in America." I have also been a pastor, promoter of organ and tissue donation, and a full time caregiver. Currently, I am back in Americus, Georgia, ministering to dying patients and their families as a full time hospice chaplain.

My home, the Shady Rest in Americus, Georgia, 1974

My Love Letter to
the Black Community

(Because It Was Written With Love)

One of the weirdest courses I ever took was taught by a former nun at a Unitarian seminary in Berkeley. It was one of the nine schools comprising Graduate Theological Union of which my school, Pacific School of Religion, was a member.

At the time, I remember thinking this woman had been smoking way too much weed, for while other professors came to class with lengthy lecture notes and lists of books for us to read, she had us put aside our notebooks and pens and do watercolors while she spoke to us about life. "Behold the options," she'd say, holding up two pieces of paper, one a clean, fresh sheet with nothing on it and another with word after word crossed out and written over. "Which is scarier for the writer?" she asked. "It's the clean sheet isn't it?" "Get in there and make a mess," she intoned, "for until you give yourself permission to screw things up, you'll never have the courage to attempt anything of significance."

As I look back, her class probably taught me more than many of the others combined for she encouraged her students to look at life from different perspectives. "Remember the chakras," she'd say, "Don't assume everyone is operating on the same chakra." Chakras, according to Eastern thought, are energy centers or zones located throughout the body. The higher the chakra, the more the emphasis is on things of the mind, the intellect, while the lower chakras stimulate the carnal, sensuous aspects of our being. Ideally, we should access all of these energy fields and not fixate on one region to the exclusion of others. Having said that, the reason, according to this system of thought, blacks are such great athletes and able to produce such soulful passion is their unique ability to access the deeper energy zones or chakras. Indeed, where would Gospel music, Jazz and Motown be without the contribution of blacks? They'd be stifled and dry, like New Orleans dialed back to the rhythmic equivalent of a Tulsa, Oklahoma.

You, my friends, are the seasoning that adds flavor to the stew and rescues us from the blandness of dull intellectual pursuits, the seductress that ignites the animal in us thereby making the domain of pleasure all the more pleasurable lest lives be lived only from the neck up. You are authentic, rooted in your humanity, the melodic voice that moves the entire body, the soulful emotion that weeps and wails loudly at funerals while others sit in stunned silence.

This is your contribution, your essence, a reminder to the rest of us that things of the heart are deep, beyond mere words the tongue can utter. The inherent risk of getting to these levels is, of course, that of getting stuck there or, even worse, being like the submarine that, unable to pull up from its descent, continues to dive until it reaches "crush depth," where it implodes into a thousand pieces.

Fifty years after Martin Luther King's March on Washington, I am profoundly saddened to hear so many in the black community now take pride in referring to themselves as "niggers, gangsters and thugs." This is not, mind you, like the practice of police departments that have taken the hate filled term "pigs" and reversed its meaning by saying it stands for P.I.G.S. or Police in Good Service. To the contrary, this is just the opposite. It is an affirmation of the very worst aspects of the designation.

I am particularly miffed at the entertainment industry. When I was a youngster looking at a map of the continental United States, I took it to resemble the picture of a dinosaur. Perhaps this is because, at the time, Sinclair Oil Company used a rough rendition of a dinosaur in their company emblem. Think about it. The head and eyes of the dinosaur are Washington, D.C. The front legs are the state of Florida, the hind legs that provide the power are Texas, the heart or bread basket is the mighty Midwest and just below where a tail would be attached is, what else, but Hollywood...thus explaining the excrement that it has put out in recent years. Tell me I am out of line here! I don't think so. They have taken impressionable youths and foisted upon them degenerate role models. This is particularly the case in the music industry where rap artists glorify guns and the gangster lifestyle, both of which are dead end streets.

Just within my brief lifetime, they have gone from producing such insightful, uplifting works of Sidney Poitier in "The Lilies of the Field" and "In the Heat of the Night" to sinking to giving an Academy Award for best music in 2006 to "It's Hard Out Here for a Pimp." That's quite a decline from "Raindrops Keep Falling on My Head", the winner in the same category in 1969.

I am old enough to remember that the best argument for segregation was that it was the only way the white community had to insulate itself from the guns, the drugs, and violence that at the time seemed endemic to the black community. Fortunately, this argument was trumped by the best argument for integration, namely that segregation closed the door to the countless number of good and decent people who were wrongly associated with such behaviors and had the right to themselves flee and live in better surroundings.

My fear is that with so many claiming the term "niggers" and identifying themselves as thugs and gangsters, this will only serve to justify a return to a negative racial profiling of the black community as a whole. I am sure that many in the white community could draw a comparison to the taking of Troy and the story of the Trojan Horse. The attackers were unable to breach the city's walls, so they constructed a massive wooden horse on wheels, left it outside the gates and drew back. Seeing that the assailants had left, those inside the fortress opened the gates and pulled in the wooden statue, then closed the gates again. In the middle of the night, while the city slept, soldiers hidden inside the horse opened the trap door, let themselves down to the ground, then ran and opened the gates and signaled for the attackers to return. Before the city's residents fully realized what was happening, their assailants had flooded in through the gates and brought down the city.

My fear is that taking pride at being "in the hood" will only spark revulsion on the part of those in the white community who still have their hoods neatly tucked away in bureau drawers waiting for a justification to go back to their previous practice of racial profiling. I mean, what argument can be put forth to those who say, "You see, you see! For fifty years we have taken down all of the barriers and drawn them in; and now that they are fully integrated, they show themselves for what we have always said they were, just a bunch of 'niggers.'"

Don't believe the lies of music moguls who seek to reap rich rewards at the expense of you reaching your full human potential. You are far more gifted, talented and able than sinking to the lowest forms of human behavior they wish to pin on you. Think about it, the word "rap" is used in only three places, all of them negative. First, there is taking the "rap" or blame, then there is a "rap sheet" that is slang for a criminal record and lastly, there is "rap music" which is a misguided glorification of antisocial behaviors that will eventually lead to your imprisonment and/or destruction. Rise up and seize the opportunities that are there for you, for me, for each of us. God has provided the ladder. It is now up to each of us to climb it. Own your soulful passions, but do not let them own you. Reach for the stars. We need you. We need each other.

And remember, if you seek to fit into any mold, be conformed in mind and spirit not to those who seek their own selfish goals at your expense, indeed your very freedom. Instead, run with absolute abandon to the other end of the spectrum, to the headwaters of limitless grace and ultimate success, to a love that does not drain or diminish, but rather from a posture of absolute sufficiency seeks only for you to know, to experience, to adopt for yourselves the truest of joys that can only be found in blessing each person and each situation you encounter. This is my deepest and highest prayer, not only for you, but also for me and for all of us. Be well.

The Death Knell of
the Human Spirit

From many years of trying to help others, I am more convinced than ever that there is only one surefire way to destroy people. Just assure them that regardless of whatever they do or don't do, they'll never go without. Then sit back and watch lives that should have thrived on ambition and determination disintegrate into idle self-destruction. It's been the ruin of many born into opulent wealth from time immemorial and now, in an equally misguided understanding of love and charity, we ladle out copious amounts of the same poison to children born into poverty.

Consequences in life are difficult to handle, yet without them we have no measurement, no scorecard to tell us if we're on track or off course. Softening life's realities by cushioning its blows might work in the short term, but what's going to happen when we aren't there to superimpose our concept of what reality should be on top of what reality already is?

Show Me a Life
Without Consequences,
and I'll Show You
An Inconsequential Life

Why We Call Bad Decisions "Poor Choices"

- If I decided to not finish high school, let alone college and graduate school, would I not have made a "poor choice" that would have greatly reduced my standard of living?

- If I decided to goof off on the job or not show up at all, would I not be making a "poor choice" resulting in me scrambling to find a new source of income?

- If I chose to ignore the law and decided instead to consume illegal drugs and/or large amounts of alcohol, would I not be making a "poor choice" that might cost innocent lives as well as my personal freedom?

- If I decided to have sex without proper birth control, would I not be making a "poor choice" that would require massive amounts of money to adequately support the children I produced?

Two More Questions:

- Is it ethical to pass the cost of these "poor choices" onto those who didn't make them?

- Isn't it responsible accountability by all that makes possible "liberty and justice for all?"

I believe that the most insidious form of child abuse is anything that denies a child their rightful progression to adulthood.

Parents who do their kids' homework while the youngsters go out to play are setting them up to fail. So, too, is a society that enables people to grow up to become perpetually irresponsible.

Public Assistance
Is About Assisting

Public assistance was never intended to assume ownership of other people's lives and their problems nor was it created to smother folks with disempowering pity. To the contrary, it was created to help people get on their feet. The problem is that we have tended to confuse lift chairs with recliners. Though they may look the same, their functions couldn't be further apart. One is designed to help one recline while the other is designed to help one stand. The first takes a person and tilts them back until they are completely at rest. The latter takes a person from a position of rest and lifts them up until they are on their feet. But it doesn't stop there. It keeps on going until it dumps the person forward, leaving them only two choices-to stand or fall flat.

The Example of
my Childhood

I was blessed with the world's greatest mother, ever! Sorry, global population, but don't feel bad; you really never had a chance as there never really was any competition. That being said, during my earliest years, she was away for protracted periods of time due to issues that were eventually resolved.

Anyway, with the very best of intentions, my brother and sister moved themselves into the spot of taking care of their youngest sibling even though we were each only 15 months apart in age. Like most toddlers and adolescents, I craved the love that came my way as a result of being their little work in progress and thrived on the attention they gave me. If I wanted sugar for my cereal or jelly for my toast, I'd barely look that way and they'd run and fetch it. It was great!

There was a downside, however. They hovered so closely that they were actually finishing my sentences before I had a chance to get my words out. In due course, I looked to them to accomplish anything and everything and never ventured out myself.

By the time they went off to school, I had become so dependent on them that I wouldn't dream of turning on the television set as they were the ones who always did it. The same was true about eating fruit. My brother and sister thought nothing of grabbing an orange or tangerine whenever they wanted it, peeling it and gobbling it down, but I had become so accustomed to going to them and having them feed me that I went without if they didn't provide for me.

Now notice, no one ever diagnosed me as being deficient in any way, but their overzealous love for me put me in such a weakened position, a position of perpetual dependence that now, fifty some years later, I still at times have to break through it just to stand on my own. And this is exactly what the well intentioned among us do with the "poor" and "disadvantaged."

We place them in a false reality where the copayment for medication is 50 cents, doctor's visits and hospitalizations are basically free and public housing is a far cry from the days of "the projects". Then, we sit back and wonder why initiative is lacking.

Just as I was saved by my brother and sister going to school, so, too, the "poor" among us would best be served by us going back to school on this one. We do them no favors by taking healthy, intelligent human beings and reducing them to virtual wards of the state. They will not only get on their feet, but reach for the stars if we would just stop providing incentives that keep them stuck in their dependency.

The problem with our way of helping is that it:

1) Assumes inability on the part of the recipient.

2) It limits growth as it threatens to withdraw at the first signs of independence.

3) Leaves the recipient weaker and more vulnerable than before we intervened, as the skills and strengths that were present at birth slowly atrophy (lose strength) due to a lack of usage. This eventually renders the person less able to function independently.

A Fatal Flaw in the War on Poverty

No matter how one slices and dices it, the fact remains that to achieve success in life, we need two ingredients: "opportunity" and "responsibility".

Opportunity was sorely lacking fifty years ago when the Rev. Dr. Martin Luther King, Jr. led the March on Washington. Thankfully, it is a very different story today. All kinds of barriers have been broken down and doors have been opened. We as a society, as a nation, are better for it.

Responsibility can be defined as owning the opportunities that life gives us and working with them to improve our situation. Where the "War on Poverty" got off track was when it took opportunity and made it into something entirely different, namely "entitlement." People have been led to feel "entitled" to guaranteed incomes, increasingly nicer and nicer housing, free health care and the like, whether or not they take advantage of the opportunities given them or not.

The Constitution guarantees citizens equal access to opportunities. It does not and cannot guarantee these opportunities will yield the same results for all because we each bring our own set of gifts, talents and baggage to whatever we attempt in life.

We've Set Out on the Ultimate Fool's Errand

While the rest of society knows that the key to success is an investment of time and energy coupled with a certain amount of risk, the poor have been given the message that they somehow live in a different reality where the blessings continue regardless of whether they are industrious or not.

It shouldn't take a Nobel Prize in Economics to recognize the underlying premise of any economy is that everyone is operating with the same system of rewards and the same carrots in front of everyone's horses. To do otherwise and set up an alternative framework where whole segments of a population are working with a different set of financial assumptions is to embark on a fool's errand. It is every bit as ridiculous as having runners in the same race set off in divergent directions for different finish lines.

Yet, that is exactly what we have in this country today. For while the majority of us have been raised with the understanding that the harder one works the better quality of life one is able to enjoy and the nicer the neighborhood one is able to live in, millions of others are proving every day that the exact opposite is true for them. We all know of untold numbers of situations where people basically goof off, "hang out" and sabotage opportunity after opportunity and still can count on getting a monthly check in the mail.

As a result, some, certainly not all, but quite a few are content to stay where they are or fall even further behind lest they lose the "benefits" to which they have been repeatedly told they are entitled.

The folly in this is that by always cushioning their fall, we have taken away the initiative that is essential to growth. We are no different than the parent that fights all of their kid's battles and takes on all of their challenges. It may satisfy the parents' need to feel helpful, but make no mistake about it, this dynamic denies the child a crucial component of their development.

At some point, no matter how benevolent and generous people choose to be, this enabling will have to stop once those who rise to an alarm clock and go to work reach the end of their collective credit limit and society as a whole is no longer able to borrow the money to keep the handouts going. What will happen then? What on earth will become of the poor?

The following are photographs of government subsidized housing in my neck of the woods.

Some units are detached, some are duplexes and others are condominium-like in appearance. All are immaculately landscaped and maintained by ground crews.

Assignment:

Drive around your neighborhood. Find housing complexes with the HUD symbol on the sign. The HUD symbol is identical in shape to the plastic Monopoly game piece that one places on the board to charge rent to those who land on owned property. The only difference is that the outline of the HUD house has an = sign drawn inside of it.

You'll be shocked to see that many are strikingly attractive mission style homes or apartment complexes with "cultured stone" facades, "architectural style" shingle roofs and new or newer cars parked out front. They have been placed in middle or even upper class neighborhoods as a way to doing away with the "stigma" of public housing.

We Need To Stop Thinking
These People Are Helpless

We are now approaching fifty years since President Lyndon Johnson declared a war on poverty. The impoverished children of the 1960's are now grandparents or, in some cases, great grandparents themselves. I doubt very much that MLK and LBJ ever intended to create a permanent welfare class. Instead, they merely wanted to give folks the opportunity to attain the full potential that already existed within them.

Example of a Rowing Coach Empowering the Team

When a rowing team is doing poorly, the coach doesn't climb into the boat, grab the oar and instruct the rowers to sit back and go for a ride while he starts pulling on the oar. No! He or she starts yelling words of encouragement from the shoreline and starts putting into play exercises that will help the team get the proper conditioning that is necessary to start pulling ahead. Our problem is that with the best of intentions, we do just the opposite. We tell people they can't do it alone, and in so doing, we unwittingly make them all the more dependent.

Why Independence and Freedom Are Interchangeable

Listen to the language. See how often our founding fathers and later voices such as the late Rev. Dr. Martin Luther King, Jr. have used the above mentioned words interchangeably when speaking of political freedom and human liberation. The reason is simple. People cannot truly be free until they establish their independence and self-sufficiency. As long as they have to depend on others, they are not autonomous, but controlled by them and subject to their bidding.

We should have people in publicly subsidized housing continue to pay the same amounts they have always paid, but starting immediately, these folks will go from renters to homeowners. This way, people who would never qualify for a home loan otherwise, will start to build up equity that will translate into a nest egg for when they retire.

The only stipulation is that the government will immediately get out of the housing business. No longer will our society attack problems in reverse. Gone will be the days of us looking at the number of children in a family and then deciding how many bedrooms to provide for them. It doesn't work that way for wage earners; why should it work that way for non-wage earners? No, from here on out, a person will have to either limit the number of children they bring into the world or increase their income to be able to care for them. Currently, the people least able to feed their children are the ones most likely to bear them. That is backwards and only perpetuates cruel, multi-generational poverty that blesses no one, least of all the children born of it.

Lest people profit from our charitable acts: Occupants will only be able to sell and keep the proceeds from these homes when one of two things happen: (1) the total cost of the unit has been paid in full, or (2) the person reaches retirement age and takes out the equity they have built up as they move into a retirement setting. Prior to paying off the cost of the home, all proceeds from the sale of these units will be automatically reapplied to the purchase of another home until the same conditions are met.

These are good, solid, first steps toward true autonomy. They are essential, for if there is one thing history tells us, it is that the feelings of the crowd are fickle. The same people that shout hosanna one day may well be in an entirely different mood, but a few days later. Be grateful for what is given you, but don't rely on it. It's best to make your own way and be dependent on no one.

We Should Take a Good Hard Look at Our Financial Aid System

1) ***Under existing programs, we have people who are skilled at having us care for them.*** If we reduce the amount of assistance we offer,

they just lower their standard of living. If we create massive labyrinths of regulations complete with checks and balances to make sure the money is going to its intended purpose, they become adept at "working the system" instead of ever actually working.

2) ***All of this goes on while other people suffer a major crisis and don't qualify for help.*** They need immediate intervention, but they don't meet the criteria for public assistance as the equity in their home classifies them as having too many assets to receive our help. These individuals have to first lose everything including their house that they have spent an entire lifetime acquiring before our charitable arm swings into action.

This is as ludicrous as it is unfair. It all boils down to this. Folks whose only visible means of support is the government might not own their place of residence, but they have even more security than those of us who do. For while the average wage earner is but a paycheck away from default on their home loans, those who are idle and have been for years are guaranteed perpetual shelter. Not only that, they are also shielded from the headache of figuring out how to pay for costly repairs such as replacing a roof, furnace or major appliance.

Apparently it isn't enough for someone to just need help with a few medical bills. No, we aren't set up to deal with that. Instead, we wait and let them go without any kind help until they are too sick to work and lose everything. Then, instead of just meeting a simple medical need, we are saddled with a whole array of massive, complex medical needs plus the responsibility of providing both an income and housing.

This isn't only financially devastating to those who could have regained their footing with just a little help. It is also financially devastating to our entire economy as many of these recipients are then given the message to stay below certain income levels in order to continue receiving help. This makes them all the more dependent for virtually forever and leaves fewer workers in the tax base to carry the burden of more and more families. In short, our approach really and truly meets the classic definition of being penny wise and pound foolish.

Right now, there's no connection between welfare and personal responsibility

I know of a situation where one of the members of a close friend's family had a severe but manageable medical condition. The intensity of the symptoms could have been minimized to the point of being almost negligible had the individual chosen to comply with easy to follow medical advice. Unfortunately, almost from day one, this person did just about everything but follow doctor's orders. As a result, an award could have probably been won for the most repeat hospital admissions in the nation (had there been such an award), the overwhelming majority of which were entirely preventable. Indeed, this person's life provides an excellent case study of what happens when we bear ultimate responsibility for people who refuse to take any responsibility for their own lives.

In addition to the countless medical bills racked up since the onset of the disease, there was a couple of year stretch where the individual would barely return home from intensive care before repeating the same practices that put the person in the hospital in the first place. This resulted in calling yet another ambulance to transport the same individual back to the same hospital, often the same intensive care unit, where the whole cycle would start all over again. For a few years, this was repeated on an almost weekly basis.

There's little doubt in my mind that taxpayers easily spent a couple of million dollars in hospital bills alone just because of this one person's conscious decision to be medically non-compliant. In addition, this same person collected public assistance as the head of a household with children and lived in a home built by a charity.

The height of it for me, however, was when it was disclosed during a family meeting that on one occasion nobody was responding to her repeated requests for a drink of water. Undeterred, she called 911. An ambulance was dispatched and soon a nice cold bottle of water was provided by emergency responders (at taxpayers' expense).

How Can This Happen?

The answer is simple. There is nothing to stop it. Our society has been so overwhelmed by guilt for its horrific sins of the past that it has become hyperextended in its attempt to make amends. The result has been the creation of a false reality where the expense of housing, healthcare and higher education are heavily (and I mean heavily) subsidized. Even if copays for medical needs are never paid (and often times they are not) the care continues because we have engineered all of the consequences out of the equation.

As for the rest of us wage earners, regardless of how much we pay, or even offer to pay an insurance company, none of us could come remotely close to recreating this same "hospital rotation" because no policy is offered without of a system of copayments and deductibles that are just high enough to make us think twice before setting up an appointment or calling an ambulance. In short, they have made us wise medical consumers. This has saved them, us and the whole industry untold billions of dollars.

While the poor are insulated from further decline regardless of their actions, workers have to pay for everyone else's "What Ifs." Just look at their paystubs!

There's the:

- "What if I become injured on the job?" contingency covered by Worker's Comp.

- "What if I or a member of my family get sick?" contingency covered by health insurance.

- And finally the, "What if total strangers, people in the general population get sick or injured?" contingency covered by federal, state and county tax withholdings.

What Does All of This Mean?

It means the people who bear the burden for most of these benefits, the middle class, are the very ones least likely to receive them.

A Flat Income Tax, Not Sales Tax, Is the Most Fair

On the surface, a flat sales tax sounds the most equitable and fair, but it actually favors the rich because at some juncture, wealthy people purchase all they need and want. From then on, the vast majority of their earnings go into enormous stockpiles of capital, while others live paycheck to paycheck and spend just about every dollar they bring home.

It reminds me of the dilemma many of us face when shopping for a gift to give our fathers on birthdays and holidays. Idea after idea is tossed aside as we realize he already has it, and if he doesn't, it's only because he probably doesn't want it. So, we come up short, stumped by that age old question, "What do you give the man who already has everything?"

Believe it or not, there are a lot of people, not just men, who fall into this category. They have more than enough, and yet, are still pulling ahead of the rest of us in their earning power. If we only collected sales taxes, the people at the top would pay a far smaller percentage of their incomes than those who barely eek-out an existence.

While it hardly seems fair to penalize the rich for succeeding, it also isn't fair that the rich pay little or nothing. A "flat income tax" instead of a "flat sales tax" is the solution. For then, everyone would pay the same percentage of their incomes regardless of whether or not they spend the income they accrue.

Let's Back Up and
Start From Scratch

Imagine a society where, because we no longer offshore our industrial production, American workers have the opportunity to earn more than enough to support their families (as they once did) on a single paycheck. On these incomes and the incomes earned by private enterprises as well as massive corporations, the same fixed, across the board tax is collected.

A Tax System like This,
Based on Tithing,
Is Fairest

It certainly seems to work for God (and I am not being flippant here, but to the contrary, very sincere.) The way tithing works in the Judeo-Christian understanding is that a flat 10% of all income is required. This is across the board, regardless of standing. It is due off the top, before anyone gets their hands on it. The beauty of this is in its proportionality. 10% of a million bucks is just as hard for a millionaire to swallow as the 10% assessed the white collar worker and the 10% assessed the pauper. Think about it.

This Will Greatly Reduce the Cost of the IRS

This tax plan also saves a whole heap of money, and I mean a really, really big, whole heap of a lot of bunches of money by immediately simplifying our tax code. No longer will we be supporting an ever burgeoning Internal Revenue Service with its legions of accountants and tax attorneys tasked with determining which "loopholes" are legal and which are not. This step alone will save the government bazillions and bazillions of dollars in administrative costs once everyone, and I mean everyone, pays the same percentage into the system, be they rich or poor, wholesale or retail, wage earner or investor, mega corporation, or mom and pop business. If the changes that I suggest in the next few pages are implemented, then it may be possible to get down to a low, tolerable rate. Whatever it is, the percentage should be the same for each contributor.

This engages the poor and gives them a sense of ownership. As it is now, a sizeable percentage of our population couldn't care less if tax revenues are squandered. It isn't their money. Once they begin paying into it, however, then they will have the same guttural reaction that I, as a taxpayer, had when I heard an ambulance had actually been summoned because no one was heeding a plea for a glass of water. Anytime we can broaden the citizens' sense of ownership in this or any democracy, it is a good thing in and of itself.

As good, honest people, I believe the following:

- We want to encourage motivation, not complacency.

- While we don't want people to go without, we also don't want to reward irresponsible, reckless behavior.

- We want to get aid to people quickly, then have they step up to the plate and cancel it once their immediate need is met and they no longer need outside help to survive.

The Need to Start Fresh

Sometimes in life, it is much more expeditious and cost effective to back out of current approaches altogether and start fresh than it is to keep trying to make things work. It's like an airplane attempting to land. Sometimes it will come in too high or too low, too fast or at the wrong angle or pitch, and the control tower will radio the pilot with instructions to circle around and make another attempt. Or, more germane to our individual experience, it's like trying to parallel park a car. If one starts from a weird angle or distance from the curb, it is much easier to pull out of the spot altogether and start fresh all over again.

OK, Then, How Do We Help
Without Creating Dependency?

In the final analysis, the best way to assist people without stifling their God given instinct to struggle to survive is to transition them away from passively receiving that for which they have not worked. This will encourage people to make wiser choices and take personal responsibility for the paths they choose. When this happens, I believe we'll begin to see more people attain their potential as autonomous, self-directed human beings.

We Need A Happy Medium Between Life Before Roosevelt When People Could Die in the Gutter and Today When People Become Lifelong Wards of the State.

A Fresh Approach

We need to figure out a way to pry off the ceilings that for decades have stymied personal achievement and held our economy back. Think of all the people we personally know who would love to pick up a few more dollars, but don't dare because it will mean the loss of unemployment benefits, a public assistance check or place people in a tax bracket where their income goes from being a blessing to being a burden.

The sum total of all of these millions of situations easily comes to billions and billions of dollars. It's an astronomical sum. We're not only talking about the loss of all of that taxable revenue, but also the cost of continuing to support millions and millions of people who, failing to rise to the occasion, have limited themselves and, therefore, continued to depend on us to feed, clothe and house them. The cost to our GNP (Gross National Product) has been incalculable.

The Solution is Twofold

First: Eliminate Ceilings and Caps
Second: Create Contingency/Rainy Day Accounts

Some will immediately respond that without ceilings and caps there will be no reason for people to stop collecting unemployment and other benefits. To which I respond, they will stop once they realize they are only spending down or depleting money that has been steadily growing with in their own Contingency/Rainy Day Savings Accounts. This is how I see these accounts working.

Instead of having our tax dollars go into a vast pool that we can't access...why not set up a Rainy Day Savings plan that people can make withdrawals from as needed? Each taxable unit (person or company) will contribute an equal percentage from their sources of revenue. They will be automatically deducted from each paycheck with a running total showing on each paystub. From this savings pool, funds can be used for those unexpected things all of us run into.

If we get laid off from work, the funds are there to carry us for a while. If we need to finance college tuition, we have funds we can draw on. If our parent needs to go into a nursing home, then, we have access to money already set aside. If wiped out by a bankruptcy or house fire or stroke, there is money to help us get back on our feet. If these accounts are ever exhausted, the system borrows money from other accounts where those funds are not yet needed.

These personal "Rainy Day Accounts" are not automatically made accessible. Only certain specific and out of the ordinary needs qualify for making these monies available.

What About When The Rainy Day Accounts Dry Up?

The system will continue to pay out until certain thresholds are met. At these junctures, one of three things will happen. The individual will submit a reasonable action plan for repayment. If none is forthcoming, the person will be assigned a task to support the public good with the proceeds going directly to paying off the loan to the system.

If the individual is unable to come up with a feasible action plan and is physically unable to work due to justifiable medical limitations, then a forbearance can be granted to postpone or forgive the debt altogether.

Consider for a moment what happens to the mindset of people when they go from welfare recipients who have to play the role of being poor enough to continue in the program to being just like everyone else in society.

Instead of figuring out how to get more and more out of the system by being societal beggars, they now have a motivation to take control and make wise decisions. Again, just imagine what people can and will do once they see their savings grow and realize they can also add to it beyond their payroll deductions. This will foster motivation instead of the defeatist message currently given that (1) they are poor and (2) they will be penalized if they so much as make any financial progress.

The goal is to put responsibility where it belongs, not on strangers, not on the society at large, but on individuals who in this day and age have more than ample opportunities to care for themselves and their families…if they do not squander them.

If for no other reason than the well-being of the recipients, the days of codependent coddling must end and end now, before those who are currently paying all of the bills reach the end of their ropes and stop it altogether. It is far more humane to transition people to self-sufficiency while there is still ample means of support in place to aid the transition.

More Benefits of This Program

People will no longer have reason to judge the way others, particularly the poor, spend money, as ultimately, it comes out of their own pocket thanks to the sweat of their brow.

If they want to live in a run down, dilapidated residence with an enormous, top-of-the line, wide screen television in the living room, and a late model car in the driveway, so be it. It's their money and, accordingly, no one else's business to pass judgment, as long as, of course, the needs of the children and other dependents in that home are met.

Even if there are a good number of people who are truly incapacitated and qualify for forbearance on the monies they will be given plus the promise of a continual infusion of financial aid, it will be far less than the number we are currently carrying who have no expectation of either ending their dependency or repaying monies they are receiving. Yet, this is just the beginning of the true societal benefits.

Consider for a moment all of the illegal activities that "the poor" currently justify engaging in as they know that verifiable incomes such as a "real job", will mean the end of getting public assistance. In light of this, there is a whole underground economy going on as these individuals, like the rest of us, have the desire to have money in their pockets.

If we take away the incentive to hide incomes and remain poor enough (at least on paper) to get help, then we have hope of motivating people to earn and save even more. As it is now, a lot of people are telling themselves they have to engage in activities they know deep down inside are wrong as they have no other choice.

What Happens To Unused Funds?

I would propose the establishment of a timetable of five year blocks. If a person is able to maintain a percentage of savings in that account, let's say 80%, then they can withdraw 20% of it for a durable good or product. A durable good or product is here defined as something that will enhance their life in the long run. Do the math, this can add up to a sizeable amount of money. It can be applied toward the purchase of a car, the down payment on a house, the investment in a Roth IRA or a business – anything that is not an indulgence. Funds not used at the end of a life, when money is most likely needed for nursing home care etc., will be returned to the general fund.

Do you see where this is going? It singlehandedly promotes responsible behavior and financial planning, while at the same time, taking away any incentive for being a couch potato. From now on, inaction will no longer result in an automatic handout. The availability of capital grows in each worker's "Rainy Day Fund" and America is off and running once again. In short, it puts the poorest among us right where they should be, in the real world, not some fictitious reality based on the generosity of strangers that can be easily withdrawn.

In this is the affirmation of their abilities, the very thing the present system lacks. For the current underlying assumption is that the poor are never going to be able to make it on their own. It assumes they will never break the surface and be able to keep their financial heads above water. This is why we equip them with gills like a fish so that at least they won't drown under water. Once so equipped, we have doomed them to intergenerational dependence, for now their struggle is not to get back on solid ground, but rather to stay in the well-stocked pond we have artificially made for them lest they suffocate like "a fish out of water" in the real world the rest of us encounter every day.

Don't believe it? Presently the system is set up so that if a "poor person" increases their income too much, they will lose their publicly supported housing, their incredible publicly supported health care benefits and of course their monthly check and food stamps.

If we really want to reduce the number of people in poverty, we also need to:

1) Close the wage gaps. There is no way those at the top can justify making hundreds of times the salary of the the average worker, yet it goes on all of the time and must be stopped. Honest work deserves good honest pay, period.

2) Give people a chance at a fresh start. Currently, a lot of people are unemployed because they drag a police record around with them for the rest of their lives. Whatever happened to paying one's debt to society and then having a clean slate?

3) Enforce usury laws. Put a lid on outrageous interest rates charged by loan sharks and credit card companies. These keep people in financial servitude. Rein them in immediately.

4) Make it illegal to drop out of school. Just as the law now requires attendance up until the ninth grade, make it mandatory to complete high school (even if the student gets pregnant).

5) This practice of women raising children with Uncle Sam as the bread winner does little more than promote irresponsible behavior. Children

need men in their lives. Restore the role of fathers as responsible providers.

The Biggest Barriers to Affordable Healthcare:

 # 1) Insurance   **# 3) Endless Documentation**

 # 2) Attorneys   **# 4) Inflated Charges**

Just as the greatest expense in building a home is not the cost of the land, nor the materials, nor even the labor, but rather, the cost of financing the mortgage, so, too, the greatest expenses in medicine is not paying for the doctors and nurses, nor medicine and infrastructure, but rather, the costs that have literally nothing to do with actually healing the body.

What was the most expensive war?
The Cold War…
~A war that was never fought~

What is medicine's greatest expense?
Health and Liability/malpractice insurance…
Paying for what may never happen.

Background:

I remember riding down the road in the back seat of my mom's Rambler in the early 1970s listening to a discussion on the radio over whether or not to allow lawyers to advertise their services. At the time, I remember thinking to myself, "What harm could it possibly do?" Boy was I mistaken! That decision to allow the legal profession the right to grow their businesses through ad campaigns has deeply impacted all of our lives. It has added a surcharge, not at all unlike a tax, onto every human activity under the sun and transformed this nation from a right friendly place in which to live into a land of ambulance chasers complete with distrust among neighbors. It is sheer madness.

I use the word "madness" deliberately as MAD, or "Mutually Assured Destruction," was the theory that prevailed during the Cold War. In a nutshell, it basically said that as long as both sides produced weapons at roughly the same rate of speed, the world would remain safe as no one in their right mind would ever "push the button," because it would result in our "mutually assured destruction."

For years and years, this approach worked (kind of). True, no one ever did push the button, but it was the unsustainable cost of the arms race itself that ultimately did destroy one of the players.

The Soviets couldn't keep up with continually buying more and more "insurance" and so, finally, their whole system collapsed. The parallels between their plight and the escalating cost of our litigious society cannot be ignored. In both cases, enormous amounts of money are spent, but not a dime of it leads to increased goods and services. It's like paying rent. Once the money is gone, it's gone, and there is nothing to show for it.

Theoretical Benefit of Ambulance Chasers

"Lawyers keep the medical profession on its toes. They are the watchdogs protecting us from sloppy healthcare. Without them, quality would plummet" or at least, so they'd have us think. In reality, lawyers have diverted a lot of time, energy and money away from medical care to protecting doctors from the very same threat of litigation lawyers have themselves created.

Today, a doctor's biggest financial expense is medical malpractice insurance, and a practice's biggest expenditure of time is on charting designed not so much to heal the patient as much as it is to prevent lawsuits. Additionally, the biggest motivation for excessive tests, scans and lab work is the fear of litigation. This all adds up to what we now call "defensive medicine."

Lawyers' unquenchable thirst for more and more business has taken their "get rich through litigation" campaigns beyond doctors, hospitals, and nursing homes to pharmaceutical companies and medical device manufacturers as well. As a result, the across the board cost for every aspect of health care has skyrocketed. Even if we don't run up expensive medical bills ourselves, Uncle Sam does by virtue of being the biggest healthcare consumer. Each month, the treasury sends out literally billions to cover these costs.

The theory behind "ambulance chasers" is that medical practitioners will, out of fear of massive judgments, provide the very best care possible. It sounds reasonable until one realizes the primary response to fear is not so much providing better care to others as much as it is providing better protection for one's self. Accordingly, resources have been reallocated away from patient care to the funding of higher medical liability coverage, increased documentation, and the prescribing of more and more lab work.

Under The Current System

Only the most obvious cases of medical neglect and malpractice with the potential for big money settlements glean the attention of attorneys. All of the other cases worthy of review are never granted a hearing. This is like having a hospital that only treats lucrative cancer and heart attack cases, but passes up on everything else.

Non-medical people (lawyers) try medical cases before other non- medical people (jurors). This makes perfect sense if the intention is to appeal to the emotions in order to win bigger verdicts, but it makes little sense if the objective is to actually improve medical care. Court verdicts might impact wallets, but seldom impact a physician's ability to practice medicine. Even if a license is suspended, a doctor can move to another state and start over.

A local attorney is currently advertising that he has collected over $420 million dollars in damages. That's nearly half a billion dollars! Now, remember that is just one law office here in SW Georgia.

Multiply that by all of the law firms nationwide in the same line of work and watch the amounts skyrocket.

Finally, factor in all of the money bilked out of the system by drug manufacturers and medical supply companies. Drugs manufactured here cost American consumers infinitely more than anywhere else in the world. Why? It is because they can get away with it. Uncle Sam will pay just about any bill that is submitted...even when it is blatantly clear that the figures are grossly inflated.

As one who has spent many years in the medical field, first, promoting organ and tissue donation and as a hospice chaplain, I can tell you that fear of litigation is the last thing that we want in medicine. In its presence, opportunities for real improvement are squandered and already limited resources are diverted from patient care to excessive documentation. Hours upon hours upon hours are diverted from caring for patients and re-allocated to diminishing the threat of potential litigation.

I firmly believe that the solution to better health care starts with an agreement. I'd just bet that if only lawyers promised to stay out of medical settings, doctors and nurses would only be more than happy to stay out of their courtrooms. It's just that simple!

Other Ways to Improve Healthcare

Currently, we limit the number of hours a pilot can be in a cockpit or a tractor trailer driver can be behind the wheel, but there are no regulations for how long a person can be on shift as a physician.

Part of the standard medical training is to be a "resident" at a hospital. What a descriptive term! It says it all. These students are required to work virtually round the clock and basically reside at the hospital with virtually little or no sleep. We then expect them to make sound, rational life and death decisions for caseloads of patients that would confound even the most seasoned of physicians.

Is that smart? These students are just becoming acquainted with the conditions they are now thrust into dealing with and expected to write prescriptions when many of them are too tired to even drive a car. I could see it if they were being trained to serve in a combat setting where replacements might be 36 hours away, but this isn't the case. Instead, it is hospitals cashing in on the savings they get by virtue of stretching physicians past the normal limits of human endurance. It's bad medicine, plain and simple.

In a similar vein, we all know of doctors who take on more patients then they can handle. For example, I am acquainted with a number of physicians who have assumed roles as medical directors of this, that and the other plus run their own sprawling medical practices plus, plus, plus. The way they do it is simple, they have their nurse practitioners and physician assistants do a lot of the work under their moniker. The fee they charge is just the same, but the consumer gets a less qualified practitioner seeing them.

In every endeavor there eventually comes into play a law of diminishing returns and I think healthcare is too important to not address this issue. Public safety demands it.

Nursing Homes

These facilities collect astronomical amounts of money whether the care is compassionate and delivered in a timely manner or not. Families who depend on them are often placed in the awful position of watching their loved ones suffer because some, certainly not all, but some of the staff members are not oriented toward compassion and mercy. Rather, they are frighteningly able to tune out patients who are calling out for their help. They act as though they don't see the obvious and can't hear reasonable requests for help.

Why does this go on? Why do patients and family members feel so powerless? It's because payment doesn't come directly from them. Rather it comes through their insurance, Medicare or Medicaid. Once these bureaucracies get a bill, the facility is paid even if the care is lousy by any standard.

I have been in nursing homes for most of my vocational career and I believe the answer is simple. It is having the facility become directly accountable to the people they serve. How does this happen? Empower recipients and their families to do what customers do in every other situation, namely pay only for the services rendered. Let me explain...

I think nursing homes should automatically get 90% of what they charge. That's a given. The remaining ten percent will be sent if and only if for that calendar month, the facility gets a 60% or better favorability rating by the people they serve. (That's more than fair as 60% would translate into a D in academic circles.)

The rating will be determined by an anonymous survey conducted by an independent organization with no vested interest on either side of the fence. The payment will be for the remaining 10% or nothing. Slicing it down into smaller percentages will only detract from the facility's urgent desire to do whatever is necessary to improve patient care and to do it quickly.

We now have patients with spotless charts and soiled sheets. Why? It is because health care is so busy operating on the negative energy of fear of lawsuits that it has neither the time nor the resources to focus on healing.

Universal Health Care? Dealing With the "Yeah, Buts…"

Like it or not, universal healthcare is already here (and has been here for some time) as evidenced by the fact that it is illegal for hospitals to deny medical care to anyone. The dollars are already being spend.

The question is, do we want our money to continue to go to insurers, lawyers and pharmaceutical giants or do we want to heal the sick, all of the sick and nothing but the sick... and do it all for much, much, much less money than the sum total we as a society currently spend on supposed "health care?" We can easily afford to pay for present realities, it is the fear of the "what if's" that is bankrupting us.

The Biggest Fear that Holds Us Back From Reaping the Benefits:

Yeah, but once you bring in everyone, you include people who have very little to contribute and who are most likely have an extensive backlog of medical problems that, in short order, will bankrupt the whole system.

Rebuttal: On the surface, it would seem so, but as mentioned earlier, all insurance carriers have built in mechanisms specifically designed to prevent this exact same thing from happening. They are called deductibles and co-pays. This requirement of making patients pay a portion of the cost for services rendered could be included in universal healthcare so that it is protected from frivolous over-usage.

Think about it. There are a lot of things I'd love to have medically checked out, but don't dare because I don't want to pay the deductible. Accordingly, I now think long and hard before running to the doctor, ER or even calling an ambulance. It is because even though I am fully insured, the costs not covered by my medical insurance (deductibles and co-pays) are high enough to make me a wise and frugal medical consumer. We can build the same co-pays into any universal plan we create, thereby protecting it from the same threat of needless over usage.

Again, whether we like it or not, we as a society are already paying for universal health care. The question is, what is the quality of that care and could we get more bang out of our buck if such a high percentage of it wasn't first siphoned off by non-medical opportunists.

In conclusion,
Why We're Out of Kilter,
Fixing America's Feng Shui

Feng Shui, the Chinese study of energy fields, speaks directly, I believe, to what is going on in our country today. It suggests that we have unwittingly set up opposing lines of energy that hinder virtually all we currently attempt in this our *United* States of America.

I mean, really, just look at us. Our political parties have divided us right down the middle and polarized us so much that most Americans think, act and vote as if our enemies are not external, but rather the other half of our fellow citizens. A perfect example of this is Bush I writing off half of the electorate by routinely referring to them as "the L word"...a group of people too profane to even mention. Talk about oppositional energy!

Then look at our societal response to poverty. We trap people in "the system" by seducing them with the message that what they need to do isn't pull ahead, but rather remain poor enough to keep on receiving assistance. *Remaining helpless enough to get help?* Look at that for just a moment. The very logic contained therein couldn't be more oppositional if it tried.

Finally, there's our motivation for health care. We have developed an entire medical system based on the ultimate application of grotesque oppositional energy. It goes like this. We will receive good care, not because anyone cares about us; no, love and compassion have nothing to do with it. We will receive good care because if we don't get it, we'll turn around and sue the pants off of those who should have provided it. What better example could there be of trying to get what we want, not by positive initiation, but rather the heartless application of oppositional energy.

None of this is working! I plead with each and every one of you, don't succumb to the lie that we as common, everyday citizens are powerless to turn this thing around. Those who have painted us into this corner want us to believe it. They want us to believe that we have no option, but to return them to power as only they have the necessary experience to govern.

Baloney feathers! We have had plenty of experience. We've experienced them taking a perfectly strong, healthy and robust country and drive it into the ground. The founding fathers had no experience with running a democracy, it was all new to them. But they had one thing that the powers that once ruled them never came close to having, a vision of and a hunger for a government of the people, by the people and for the people.

A Simple 10 Point Plan
to Rescue America

1) *Elect a decisive President who is truly independent and not tied in to either party.*

2) *Have him/her work to reduce the influence of political parties.*

3) *Get rid of all lobbyist loot. Have the government allocate 100% of all election funds with a reasonable budget given each campaign.*

4) *Illegalize deal making in passing legislation. Make it just as illegal to buy or trade votes in Congress as it is on Election Day.*

5) *Make every citizen's vote truly count. Dump the Electoral College.*

6) *Stop being chicken! Stand up to China before it is too late!*

7) *Make America our most favored nation. Reopen our factories now.*

8) *Be the very best of neighbors to Mexico. Send them ridiculous amounts of foreign aid, but don't legitimize illegal immigrants.*

9) *Establish the same rights and obligations to all citizens.*

10) *Get past the guilt trips. Enjoy life, liberty and the pursuit of happiness.*

LIST OF HEADINGS